LONDON BUS FILE 9

SINGLE DECKERS

KEN GLAZIER

Capital Transport

INTRODUCTION

This is one of a series of handbooks, each of which contains a complete list of all buses and coaches owned by London Transport during a period of between four and six years, together with a brief description and history of each type covered. Vehicles which either joined or left the fleet during the period under review are listed with additional columns showing the dates on which they were formally taken into or removed from stock. These refer to the dates when ownership changed and, in the case of buses taken out of stock, do not necessarily coincide with the day a vehicle left London Transport's hands physically. Vehicles sold were often despatched before the paper work was completed and some vehicles were stored for a time after being sold. Where a body was scrapped before its chassis, the day on which the body was scrapped is deemed to be the date the complete vehicle was written off. For vehicles bodied by manufacturers other than London Transport, the date into stock is the date when the completed vehicle was first received from the body builder. The chassis will have been owned for some time before this as the normal procedure was for the chassis to be delivered formally to London Transport, either physically or as a book transaction, before being sent for bodying. For vehicles bodied at Chiswick, the date into stock is the date when the body was officially recorded as having been mounted on the chassis.

Although most of the single-deckers acquired by the LPTB came directly from the LGOC or its associated companies, they were not nearly so dominant as in the double-deck fleet. A total of 1,489 single-deckers were acquired between 1933 and 1935, of which 883 were from Combine companies and 606 from other operators. Most of the buses that came from Combine companies were of standard types, the largest types being the T (377) and LT (202) with smaller numbers of ADC, AW, R, DA and BN types, as well as 58 of the oldest, the S class, and one of the newest, the Q. In contrast those acquired from other operators comprised 31 different makes of chassis, as well as many more different models within those chassis types. The largest single make was the Gilford (GF and GD classes), of which the Board acquired 222, so becoming the largest ever operator of the make. There were also significant numbers of Dennis E, Leyland Titan and Leyland Tiger, all of which were large saloons. The next largest chassis make after Gilford was Dennis, many of which were small saloons. The wealth of small buses included in the total represents the different style of operation in the country area, the source of nearly all of the non-standard single-deckers, the number of single-deckers coming from London Area Independents being few. Many of these small buses were operated on frequent urban services in areas such as Grays, Slough and Windsor, St Albans and Watford. London Transport took early action to replace these with double-deckers, including some transferred from Central Buses where they were surplus to requirements. For services which needed small buses, the Board gave priority to ordering a new small single-decker to replace the less satisfactory examples and the first order they authorised was for the Leyland Cub. The older large saloons were replaced by successive orders for the Q class, which was at first adopted as standard but the 1936 replacement programme for Green Line coaches included the 9T9s and the main programme to replace the first generation Green Line coaches (T, TD and TR classes) was again based on the AEC Regal (10T10). The Private Hire coaches from the same period were replaced by the new LTC class in 1937/1938. Pointers to the future possible course of vehicle policy were the batches of TF coaches and CR omo buses in 1939, following the operation of the two prototypes, but the war interrupted further developments, which took a different course in post-war years.

These books would not have been possible without the unstinting help of Dr Andrew Gilks, from whose private collection the bulk of the information concerning dates has been derived. He has also done much donkey work, beyond the call of duty, in sorting out a great deal of the detail regarding specifications of individual buses. One important point needs to be made here. No vehicle records were kept by London General Country

First published 2002   ISBN 185414 262 3
© Capital Transport Publishing, 38 Long Elmes, Harrow Weald, Middlesex

Services from its formation in 1932, nor by its successor the Country Bus and Coach department between 1933 and 1935. For these years it has been necessary to rely on the records kept in the Peter Wilson archive and on those published by the PSV Circle in its supplements LT6 and LT6A. This data varies in detail but is all that is available and we must be grateful that these sources exist. Even so, there are a few vehicles whose fate cannot be traced for certain after 1932 and which may or may not have been taken over by the LPTB. These are acknowledged in the text. Two important sources of vehicle information have been *London Buses*, vols 1 and 2 (Blacker, Lunn, Westgate) and John Aldridge's *British Buses Before 1945*. Thanks are also due to John Gent, Malcolm Papes and David Ruddom for providing so many of the illustrations from their personal collections and to the photographers of the time, who are acknowledged separately in the body of the book. The two names that appear most often are D.W.K. Jones and J.F. Higham, without whose pioneering work we would all be much the poorer.

CONTENTS

Title page **Nineteen of the legendary Leyland Lion PLSC3 became part of the LPTB fleet, eleven from London Area Independents, where single-deckers of any kind had been a rare commodity. LN 4 was typical of most in having a Dodson 32-seat rear-entrance body and had been the only single-decker in the fleet of Empress Motors of Bethnal Green who ran it on route 202. It remained on that route in LPTB ownership, allocated to Old Kent Road garage, and is seen freshly turned out in its new livery at Surrey Docks Station.**
J.F. Higham collection

Front cover **Prototype Cub C1 in rural Surrey.** Painting by Glyn Kraemer-Johnson

S

The S-type was an enlarged version of the K, introduced in 1921 following an increase in the maximum permitted gross weight from 7 to 8½ tons, a concession which had been sought by the LGOC. It was nearly two feet longer than the K, at 24ft 8¼ inches, with a wheelbase of 14ft 11ins. This enabled the double-deck version to have fifty-four seats, only two short of the figure which was later to be the standard for nearly thirty years up to the 1950s. Sixty-four solid-tyred single-deckers were built between 1922 and 1924, fourteen of which were for operation by the National Omnibus and Transport Co. on behalf of the LGOC. A further fourteen were added to the National total in 1927, this time with pneumatic tyres (S 901, 915–927). The original sixty-four were fitted with pneumatic tyres in 1928 and those remaining in use in 1932 were fitted with enclosed driver's cabs and glass windscreens.

Replacement of the S single-deckers was started by the LGOC with the T and LT classes and although fifty-eight remained in stock when the LPTB was formed, many of them were delicensed. The class enjoyed a brief Indian summer between 1933 and 1936, when additional large saloons were needed to stock new routes and to convert routes from one-man-operation, but they were then replaced by the new 5Q5s. The class last ran in service on route 230 from Harrow Weald garage, where the last eight were delicensed on 17th June 1936.

Chassis:	AEC 401
Engine:	AEC 5.1 litre 35 bhp petrol
Transmission:	3-speed chain gear with spur reverse
Bodywork:	LGOC (Chiswick); or Short Bros. (S 382, 386, 442, 447, 472, 524, 776, 780, 836, 842, 872, 878, 902)
Capacity:	B30R
L.T. codes:	Not allocated
Built:	1921 (S 327–892 range); 1927 (S 915–927)
Number built:	78
Number in stock:	1.7.33: 58 31.12.39: Nil Last out of stock 7.1.37

S		Date out of stock	S		Date out of stock	S		Date out of stock
327	NK4473	29.7.36	472	XL8798	4.7.35	881	XO4079	15.7.35
369	XL3779	11.12.36	512	XL718	27.10.36	887	XO4095	14.12.36
371	XL3780	14.12.36	516	XL723	4.7.35	889	XN1765	31.7.35
377	XL3800	27.10.36	524	XM730	6.7.35	890	XN1757	27.10.36
379	XL3789	3.7.35	531	XM738	27.10.36	892	XN1781	27.10.36
382	XL3791	29.7.35	776	XO4096	4.7.35	915	YH1101	*
384	XL3792	s 1.1.35	780	XO4097	4.7.35	916	YH1102	*
386	XL3794	23.10.36	822	XO4067	18.7.35	917	YH1103	*
391	XL3798	6.7.35	833	XN1782	15.7.35	918	YH1104	*
408	XL8920	6.7.35	835	PD5983	3.7.35	919	YH1105	*
409	XL8921	8.7.35	836	XN1783	8.7.35	920	YH1106	*
417	XL3795	3.7.35	841	PD5981	1.8.35	921	YH1107	*
423	XL8933	17.7.35	842	XO7609	6.7.35	922	YH1108	*
424	XL3793	29.7.35	858	XO4610	6.7.35	923	YH1109	*
425	XL8934	22.10.36	861	XO4072	31.7.35	924	YH1110	*
433	XL8940	29.7.36	866	XO7611	c 7.1.37	925	YH1111	*
439	XL8945	17.7.35	872	XO7612	10.8.35	926	YH1112	*
442	XL8948	24.8.36	873	XO4088	12.12.36	927	YH1113	*
447	XL8955	22.10.36	877	XO7614	3.10.34			
458	XM710	24.8.36	878	XO4073	6.7.35			

* These buses were part of the LGCS fleet and passed to Country Buses when acquired by the LPTB. No record therefore exists of their withdrawal dates but they are known to have operated until some time in 1934.
s Converted to tree lopper (later as 16S).

The S-type single-deck bodies were in effect the lower deck of the double-deck version with a short extension at the back incorporating the entrance platform. S 417 is at The Grove Hotel Dulwich on a garage run. Such workings and the operation of S-type on route 109 came to an end in January 1934 when Nunhead surrendered its weekend allocation to Elmers End, the withdrawal of these slow vehicles enabling a fifteen per cent running time reduction.
The Omnibus Society

Although near contemporaries of the double-deck NS-type, the S-type single-deckers were of an earlier generation of design, with high floors and three step entrances, as shown here on an Enfield example at Epping Forest.
D.W.K. Jones

The fourteen S-type built for operation by National in 1927 had an improved style of body similar to those fitted to the K-type. Generally more modern in appearance, they had drop-down opening windows without the separate 'hopper' type openers, a domed roof and smoother inward curving side panels. Although unnumbered in this photograph taken in Watford, the vehicle was known to Chiswick as S 923.
J.F. Higham/The Omnibus Society

DE

The E, introduced in 1925, was the first forward control model from Dennis Motors. It had a low chassis frame and pneumatic tyres as standard and was suitable for bodywork seating up to 33 passengers in a length of 25 ft and width of 7ft 1in. It was a popular model with many operators but had a short production life as it was replaced in 1930 by the Arrow and later the Lancet. There were two improved versions, which had a 6-cylinder engine, the ES and the EV.

The LPTB acquired 41 of the model. Four were taken into stock from LGCS on vesting day and seventeen more joined the Country Bus fleet when acquired from Independents between August 1933 and August 1935. None of these were ever numbered as they did not receive a Chiswick overhaul before being withdrawn. The 20 Central Bus vehicles were acquired from seven Independent operators between November 1933 and December 1934 and were numbered in the DE series which had been used by the London Public Omnibus Co. and the LGOC for similar vehicles, none of which passed to London Transport. DE 28 was given the number D 193 at first but this was probably a mistake as earlier acquisitions had been numbered as DEs immediately. It was renumbered in January 1934.

Most of the Country Bus Dennis Es were disposed of between July 1935 and May 1936 after the arrival of the 4Q4s but two of the oldest went in October 1934 and one straggler remained until September 1936. The Central Bus vehicles worked mainly on former Birch Bros route 231 from Chalk Farm garage, with four allocated to Old Kent Road for route 202. Most of those operating on 231 were replaced by spare Ts in August and October 1934 although a few were kept for operation on Saturdays when vehicle requirements were greater. Those still in service were all replaced by the 5Q5s during 1936, the last being delicensed on 29th May.

The largest single intake of Dennis Es into the LPTB fleet came from Birch Bros with that company's own bodywork, of which DE 39 was typical. They used them on route 231, whose eastern terminus was Hampstead Heath, where DE 39 was photographed soon after passing to London Transport, still in full Birch livery but with garage and running number plates and standard London Transport route number stencil on the side. It was built in 1930 and was never fitted with a driver's windscreen, the effect of this, the old-style radiator and the flight of steps up to the rear platform being to give it an appearance of greater antiquity than it merited. Ken Glazier collection

Rare Phoenix bodywork was carried by DE 24 formerly owned by E. Puttergill who had run it on route 202, as London Transport continued to do. The large route and destination indicator box (complete with badly adjusted blind) was similar to those fitted to single-deck S-type buses in the Central Area (see page 5) D.W.K. Jones

This unfussy and well-proportioned body was built by Strachan & Brown for Aldershot & District in 1927. OT4743 was one of the twenty-one Dennis Es which went into the Country Bus fleet and did not receive a fleet number but it remained, at least for a time, in its old domain in the Guildford and Dorking area. J.F. Higham/The Omnibus Society

London Transport had three Dennis EVs including this Duple-bodied 32-seat bus which came from Comfy Cars of Harpenden. It has the improved radiator design introduced at the end of the 1920s and the complete vehicle is a good-looking modern bus, let down slightly by the perforated bracket between the canopy and the front bulkhead. It stands somewhere in the Buckinghamshire countryside. J.F. Higham

Chassis:	Dennis E: except DE 25, 26 (ES), KX4337, UR4577, GF6680 (EV)
Engine:	Dennis 4-cylinder 6.24-litre 70 bhp petrol (E); 6-cylinder 6.1 litre 70 bhp petrol (ES and EV)
Transmission:	Dennis 4-speed crash
Bodywork:	Birch (DE 25, 29–40, GF6680); Dennis (OT6136, 6137, 6914); Dodson (DE 26–28, 41–43); Duple (UR4577); Phoenix (DE 24); Strachan (KX1541, 1645, 1924–1928, 2219, 2793, 2794, 4337, OT4743, PP9954) The body manufacturer of RO7267, 7649, UR914 is not known.
Capacity:	B30R (DE 24–40); B32R (DE 41, KX1541, 1924–1928, 2219, 2793, 2794, 4337, RO7267, 7649, UR914, 4577); B32F (KX1645); B32? (OT4743, 6136, 6137, 6914); B30? (PP9954); C32R (GF6680);
L.T. codes:	Not allocated
Built:	1926 (DE 28, 42, 43); 1927 (DE 29–34, 41, OT4743, 6136, 6137, 6914, RO7267, 7649); 1928 (DE 24, 27, 35–37, KX1541, KX1645, PP9954, UR914); 1929 (DE 25, 26, KX1924–1928, 2219, 2793, 2794, UR4577); 1930 (DE 38–40, KX4337, GF6680)

Number acquired: 41
Number in stock 1.7.33: 4   31.12.39: Nil   Last in stock: 5.9.36

	Acquired from		Date into stock	Date out of stock
24	UC9525	E. Puttergill (Golden Arrow), Stockwell	22.11.33	30.7.36
25	UU1907	G.H. Allitt & Sons Ltd, Rotherhithe	1.12.33	4.8.36
26	UW1417	G.H. Allitt & Sons Ltd, Rotherhithe	1.12.33	30.7.36
27	UC3013	G.H. Allitt & Sons Ltd, Rotherhithe	1.12.33	4.8.36
* 28	TW5863	Gordon Omnibus Company Ltd., Leyton	13.12.33	4.8.36
29	YT6958	Birch Bros. Ltd, Kentish Town	21.2.34	18.6.35
30	YU1015	Birch Bros. Ltd, Kentish Town	21.2.34	23.7.35
31	YU1016	Birch Bros. Ltd, Kentish Town	21.2.34	25.7.36
32	YU1017	Birch Bros. Ltd, Kentish Town	21.2.34	18.6.35
33	YU1018	Birch Bros. Ltd, Kentish Town	21.2.34	18.6.35
34	YU8159	Birch Bros. Ltd, Kentish Town	21.2.34	4.9.36
35	UC1945	Birch Bros. Ltd, Kentish Town	21.2.34	24.7.35
36	UC1946	Birch Bros. Ltd, Kentish Town	21.2.34	4.8.36
37	UC8332	Birch Bros. Ltd, Kentish Town	21.2.34	28.7.36
38	YV1227	Birch Bros. Ltd, Kentish Town	21.2.34	25.7.36
39	UL1966	Birch Bros. Ltd, Kentish Town	21.2.34	26.7.35
40	UL4420	Birch Bros. Ltd, Kentish Town	21.2.34	4.8.36
41	YF6944	Westminster Omnibus Company Ltd, Holloway	10.7.34	28.6.35
42	ML754	Prince Omnibus Company Ltd, Tottenham	4.12.34	9.7.35
43	ML2078	Prince Omnibus Company Ltd, Tottenham	4.12.34	29.7.35
†	GF6680	LGCS Ltd (formerly E.W. W.C. & R.A. Cain, Red Rover Saloon Coaches, Aylesbury)	1.7.33	10.4.36
	KX1541	The Penn Bus Company Ltd	1.8.35	5.9.36
	KX1645	Amersham & District Motor Bus and Haulage Co. Ltd	24.11.33	25.4.36
	KX1924	Amersham & District Motor Bus and Haulage Co. Ltd	24.11.33	3.2.36
	KX1925	Amersham & District Motor Bus and Haulage Co. Ltd	24.11.33	10.1.36
	KX1926	Amersham & District Motor Bus and Haulage Co. Ltd	24.11.33	21.3.36
	KX1927	Amersham & District Motor Bus and Haulage Co. Ltd	24.11.33	23.3.36
	KX1928	Amersham & District Motor Bus and Haulage Co. Ltd	24.11.33	3.2.36
	KX2219	Amersham & District Motor Bus and Haulage Co. Ltd	24.11.33	9.3.36
	KX2793	Amersham & District Motor Bus and Haulage Co. Ltd	24.11.33	7.35
	KX2794	Amersham & District Motor Bus and Haulage Co. Ltd	24.11.33	5.2.36
	KX4337	Amersham & District Motor Bus and Haulage Co. Ltd	24.11.33	6.3.36
	OT4743	Aldershot & District Traction Co. Ltd	2.8.33	17.4.36
	OT6136	Aldershot & District Traction Co. Ltd	2.8.33	15.5.36
	OT6137	Aldershot & District Traction Co. Ltd	2.8.33	10.34
	OT6914	Aldershot & District Traction Co. Ltd	2.8.33	10.34
	PP9954	Amersham & District Motor Bus and Haulage Co. Ltd	24.11.33	10.4.36
	RO7267	LGCS Ltd (formerly C. Aston, Watford)	1.7.33	15.5.36
	RO7649	LGCS Ltd (formerly C. Aston, Watford)	1.7.33	14.5.36
	UR314	LGCS Ltd (formerly C. Aston, Watford)	1.7.33	10.4.36
	UR4577	A.P. & P.B. Morgan (Comfy Coaches), Harpenden	6.2.34	3.3.36

* Numbered D 193 until January 1934.
† Numbered D 2 in the Green Line series

ASSOCIATED DAIMLER TYPES

ADC 416, 423 and 427

NOTE: These were not allocated fleet numbers officially but the Rolling Stock department at Chiswick informally numbered the LGOC-owned 416 vehicles operated by National and the two 427s as AD 1–55, which is how they have often been identified. However, as the sequence of numbers does not follow the same pattern as the registration numbers it disturbs the logic of the different blocks of vehicles. The vehicles are therefore identified by their registration numbers and the following list is arranged in registration number order with the spurious fleet numbers shown in a separate column.

The 416 model was introduced by Associated Daimler in 1927 and marked a significant step forward in single-deck bus design for London. The chassis frame was cranked over the axles and an underslung worm rear axle adopted, so that the saloon floor could be lower, though not as low built as the NS. The 416 also had a new design of four-speed gearbox mounted amidships with an inclined transmission line. Both AEC four-cylinder (416A) and Daimler six-cylinder (416D) engines were available. At first the AEC was the A119 5.1 litre unit but later deliveries for the 1928 season had the improved A127. The 423 was a Daimler Coventry-built improved version of the 416D and the 426 a Southall-built upgrade of the 416A. The 427 was a normal control model with a mechanical specification similar to the 426.

The LGOC bought fourteen 28-seat 416A coaches for its Private Hire fleet, 39 buses for operation by National and eleven buses for East Surrey, all with LGOC Chiswick-built bodywork. Four of the coaches were also allocated to National. In 1929 the fourteen coaches were fitted with bus bodies, five new from Hall Lewis and nine second-hand from R class vehicles, the 14 coach bodies being substituted for the bus type on the Reliances. This exchange was made to avoid having a mixture of Reliances and ADCs in the National fleet, when additional buses were needed in 1930. The East Surrey Traction Co. also bought fourteen 416A and five 416D buses which were fitted with LGOC bodywork. The LGOC bought only one 423 which was fitted with a 20-seat Short Brothers body and was always described as a 'Parlour Coach'. For this reason it has sometimes been described as being numbered PR 1 but there is no evidence that any such number was allocated, nor that it was Lord Ashfield's private saloon. East Surrey bought three 426s with 28-seat bus bodywork by LGOC and the LGOC bought two 427 Chiswick-bodied coaches which were later described as 18-seat buses. All were transferred to London General Country Services in April 1932 and, with one possible exception, passed to the LPTB on 1st July 1933. The exception was PH1201 for which no information exists after 1927 and it is possible that this bus did not even go to LGCS.

The Board also acquired three 416s, two bus and one coach, with the business of the Watford Omnibus Co. on vesting day and three 426 coaches, from Amalgamated Omnibus Service and Supplies Ltd (Batten's Coaches) on 23rd December 1933.

The ADCs continued in service unchanged as Country Buses until the delivery of the 4Q4s allowed their withdrawal between September 1935 and February 1936 (apart from UC2227 which was taken out of stock in February 1934, possibly following accident damage).

YU3893 ('AD 6') was one of five ADC416A buses bought in 1927 for operation by National and carried a Chiswick-built 32-seat rear entrance body. The neat styling of the new ADC radiator and the low-slung chassis help to produce a modern looking bus which makes the contemporary S-type single-deckers look positively antique. YU3893 was photographed in St Albans in its early days of operation for the LPTB. J.F. Higham/The Omnibus Society

The 32-seat ADC416A buses had a narrow entrance behind the rear wheels and a folding door at the front, which contributed to making the nearside a good deal more untidy looking than the offside. YU3894 ('AD 4') is parked in Two Waters garage which opened in April 1935, ten months before the bus was taken out of stock. Alan Cross

The 30-seat ADC416s had an open rear platform as illustrated here on UC2243 picking up in Watford. The open cab is a surprising survival but does provide the opportunity to illustrate the driver's protective apron in use, with the driver's head just visible above it. Watford garage was allocated WG when garage codes were introduced by Country Buses, who were apparently unaware of the existence of West Green, but this was later altered to WT. J.F. Higham

East Surrey had three of the AEC-designed ADC426s with the style of LGOC Chiswick-built bodywork shown on PH8881 which had migrated north by the time this photograph was taken in Chesham. The Amersham & District coach in the background became T 362 and was modified to 11T11 status in 1938. J.F. Higham

Two of these normal control ADC427s were bought as coaches by the LGOC in 1928 but were transferred to LGCS in 1932 and came to London Transport as 18-seat buses. This one was allocated to Windsor at the time of the photograph, WC having been the original, apparently misguided, choice for that garage which soon became WR. D.W.K. Jones

Chassis:	Associated Daimler 416A, 416D, 423, 426 or 427
Engine:	AEC A119 or A127 4-cylinder 5.1 litre 45 bhp petrol; or Daimler CV25 sleeve-valve 6-cylinder 3.6 litre 70bhp petrol
Transmission:	AEC 4-speed
Bodywork:	Clark (HM9327); Cowieson (FG4697); Duple (HM9650, 9651); Hall Lewis (HM 8507, UC2205–2207, 2210, 2211); Metcalfe (DR 3734); Short Bros. (UC2261); remainder LGOC
Capacity:	B18F (UC2217, 2218); B29R (UC2203–2216); B30R (FG4697, UC2222–2254, and all PH registered buses); B32R (DR3734, YU3884–3886, 3893–3895); C20R (UC2261); C28F (HM9650, 9651); C29R (HM8507); C30F (HM9327);
Built:	1927 (YU registered vehicles and PH1192–1203, 1892, 3312–3316); 1929 (HM9327, 9650, 9651); 1928 remainder
Number built:	65 (56 416; 1 423; 6 426; 2 427)
Number in stock:	1.7.33: 53 31.12.1939: Nil Last out of stock: 23.3.36

Dates into stock: All 1.7.33 except HM9327, HM9650 and HM9651 acquired from Batten's Coaches on 23.12.33.

ADC	Unofficial fleet no.	Date out of stock	ADC	Unofficial fleet no.	Date out of stock	ADC	Unofficial fleet no.	Date out of stock
416 type								
† DR3734		10.35	PH8878		8.1.36	UC2235	39	9.35
† FG4697		8.1.36	PH8879		7.1.36	UC2236	17	9.35
† HM8507		3.2.36	PH8880		11.1.36	UC2237	18	9.35
PH1192		11.35	UC2203	50	9.35	UC2238	19	12.35
PH1193		11.35	UC2204	52	9.35	UC2239	20	12.35
PH1194		by 2.9.35	UC2205	34	9.35	UC2240	48	13.2.36
PH1195		11.35	UC2206	32	9.35	UC2241	22	9.1.36
PH1196		11.35	UC2207	33	15.1.36	UC2242	24	12.35
PH1197		11.35	UC2208	51	* 12.33	UC2243	26	11.35
PH1198		11.1.36	UC2209	53	* 12.33	UC2244	25	9.35
PH1199		13.1.36	UC2210	35	9.35	UC2245	42	13.1.36
PH1200		9.1.36	UC2211	31	11.35	UC2246	23	9.35
PH1201	not known (see text)		UC2212	49	* 12.33	UC2247	40	9.35
PH1202		11.35	UC2213	28	9.1.36	UC2248	36	9.35
PH1203		11.35	UC2214	27	9.35	UC2249	43	23.3.36
PH1892		11.35	UC2215	29	* 12.35	UC2250	44	10.1.36
PH3312		9.35	UC2216	30	9.35	UC2251	47	13.2.36
PH3313		16.1.36	UC2222	7	9.35	UC2252	45	9.1.36
PH3314		9.35	UC2223	8	9.35	UC2253	41	10.1.36
PH3315		9.1.36	UC2224	9	9.1.36	UC2254	46	9.35
PH3316		11.35	UC2225	10	7.1.36	YU3884	1	13.2.36
PH8869		10.1.36	UC2226	11	10.1.36	YU3885	2	13.2.36
PH8870		12.35	UC2227	12	* 2.34	YU3886	3	6.1.36
PH8871		12.35	UC2228	16	11.35	YU3893	6	10.1.36
PH8872		12.35	UC2229	14	9.35	YU3894	4	8.2.36
PH8873		11.1.36	UC2230	15	9.35	YU3895	5	9.1.36
PH8874		12.35	UC2231	21	12.35			
PH8875		11.1.36	UC2232	13	9.35			
PH8876		7.1.36	UC2233	37	9.35			
PH8877		10.1.36	UC2234	38	9.35			

* These are shown as withdrawal dates in the Peter Wilson archive lists; they may have remained in stock longer.
† Ex-Watford Omnibus Co. (formerly Western National, W. Alexander and Batten's respectively).

423 type

UC2261		20.6.38

426 type

HM9327	10.2.36	HM9651	9.1.36	PH8882		5.2.36
HM9650	8.1.36	PH8881	27.1.36	PH8883		4.2.36

427 type

UC2217	54	14.5.36
UC2218	55	18.5.36

This style of body with a canvas section in the roof which could be rolled back in fine weather, was known as 'all-weather', hence the type code AW for this batch of ADC419 coaches built by Short Brothers of Rochester. The radiator style was specially designed for these coaches and bore some similarity to that used on the LS-type. The AWs saw little service with London Transport and AW 41 had been withdrawn for disposal when photographed in an open yard.
D.W.K. Jones

AW

These were private hire coaches on normal control chassis based on the ADC 416D but built to the specification of the LGOC, with a specially designed front end and radiator. They were classified 419. AW 9–41 were new in 1927, when they had Short Bros. 'open tourer' bodies but these were replaced by new 28-seat 'all-weather' bodies by the same manufacturer in the spring of 1930. These had canvas tops which could be rolled back, and swing passenger doors fore and aft. The fleet numbers were not carried on the coaches. Six similar Short-bodied 'open tourer' coaches were bought by the East Surrey Traction Co. in 1927 (East Surrey numbers 145, 147–151) but these were never numbered in the AW series. AW 1–8 had been withdrawn in 1929.

All 47 passed to Green Line for private hire work and then to LGCS before being acquired by the LPTB. They were withdrawn in 1934 but full details of their withdrawal dates and subsequent fate are not available as no vehicle records were kept at Reigate. The information given in the list below is based on the best information available at the time of compilation.

Chassis:	Associated Daimler 419, normal control
Engine:	Daimler CV25 sleeve-valve 6-cylinder 3.6 litre 70bhp petrol
Transmission:	LGOC 3 speed chain gearbox
Bodywork:	Short Bros.
Capacity:	28 seat 'all-weather' coach (AW 9–41); 28-seat 'open tourer' coach (unnumbered vehicles).
Built:	1927 (AW 9–41 rebodied 1930)
Number built:	55
Number in stock:	1.7.33: 47 31.12.1939: Nil

Dates into stock: All acquired from LGCS on 1.7.33. (Last out of stock 11.35)

AW		Date out of stock	AW		Date out of stock	AW		Date out of stock
9	YE4368	3.34	22	YE4381	4.34	35	YE4394	8.34
10	YE4369	.34	23	YE4382	.34	36	YE4395	3.34
11	YE4370	5.34	24	YE4383	3.34	37	YE4396	.34
12	YE4371	5.34	25	YE4384	3.34	38	YE4397	3.34
13	YE4372	3.34	26	YE4385	.34	39	YE4398	.34
14	YE4373	6.34	27	YE4386	3.34	40	YE4399	3.34
15	YE4374	3.34	28	YE4387	3.34	41	YE4400	3.34
16	YE4375	3.34	29	YE4388	5.34		PH1204	11.35
17	YE4376	3.34	30	YE4389	3.34		PH1205	2.34
18	YE4377	3.34	31	YE4390	.34		PH1206	2.34
19	YE4378	5.34	32	YE4391	3.34		PH1207	2.34
20	YE4379	5.34	33	YE4392	8.34		PH1208	2.34
21	YE4380	4.34	34	YE4393	.34		PH1209	2.34

The natural stamping ground for LS 6 was route 104 (later renumbered 240) on which it was photographed at Golders Green during its brief period of operation by London Transport. It was the only single-decker in the class and, with 34 seats, the largest operated at the time of its introduction in 1927. The styling was similar to the 1927 S-type but the extra vertical skirt panels broke the smooth inward curve and had the effect of making them look older in style. Ken Glazier collection

LS

The LS was manufactured by Associated Daimler in 1927 and was the first three-axle bus purchased by the London General Omnibus Company. Of the twelve they bought, one was a single-decker (LS 6) and this remained unique. The intended motive power was the new AEC A121 four-cylinder 7.6 litre engine but because not enough were ready in time LS 6, like most of the double-deckers, was fitted with a Daimler CV35 5.7 litre petrol engine. When new LS 6 had electric transmission similar to that used on Tilling Stevens petrol-electrics, but this was replaced by conventional transmission in 1929.

LS 6 spent its entire operational life at Cricklewood garage and, apart from an inaugural spell on route 16A (Cricklewood–Victoria), always operated on the 104 and its post-Bassom successor the 240. It was withdrawn in 1935 and its chassis used for a breakdown tender, in which capacity it remained in service until being sold in April 1951.

Chassis: Associated Daimler 802, three-axle
Engine: Daimler CV35 6-cylinder sleeve-valve 5.76 litre, 85bhp petrol
Transmission: AEC 4-speed crash
Bodywork: LGOC
Capacity: B34R
L.T. codes   Not allocated
Built: 1927
Number built: 1
Number in stock: 1.7.33: 1   31.12.1939: Nil

LS	Date into stock	Date out of stock
6	1.7.33	s 5.6.36

s Chassis used for breakdown tender (numbered 219U in 1940)

GF and GD

The Gilford Motor Co, operating from premises in Holloway Road, London, was registered on 6th November 1926, having started under the name of E.B. Horne & Co. some years earlier. Until 1925 the company had concentrated on selling reconditioned chassis, many recovered from First World War battlefields but in 1925 turned to building its own. Between then and the early 1930s, the company developed a number of models which proved to be very popular with coach operators in particular, so much so that larger premises were established in High Wycombe in 1930. In London and the Home Counties the independent companies operating the so-called suburban coach services, the predecessors of Green Line, used a substantial number, while a few others used them as buses. Many carried bodywork built by Wycombe Motor Bodies, an associated company registered in 1927 with its factory in High Wycombe. Between July 1933 and August 1934 London Transport took into stock no fewer than 220 Gilfords, the largest non-standard class in the fleet by a substantial margin, making the Board the largest ever operator of the make. The loss of the London area market was given as one of the reasons why the company eventually failed. It was wound up at the end of 1935, soon followed by Wycombe Motor Bodies.

Neither London Transport nor the LGOC, nor any of its associated companies, purchased any Gilfords new. However London General Country Services built up a total of 51 between February 1932 and May 1933, acquired from six operators they had taken over, either directly or through Green Line Coaches Ltd. These passed to the Board on vesting day 1st July 1933 together with seven from Maidstone & District. By far the largest single subsequent intake was on 10th January 1934 when 65 were acquired from Edward Hillman, running on services from Bow Road to Romford and Brentwood, and its associated company Upminster Services, running between Aldgate and Upminster. Hillman contributed another 22 when the operations centred on Bow were taken over on 13th August 1934, the longer distance services being handed over to Eastern National.

The most popular model was the 168OT, of which 148 were acquired, and the next largest, at 32, the 166OT. These were similar models, the OT code meaning 'over type' (forward control) and the number indicating 16ft 8in and 16ft 6in wheelbase respectively. Both had American-built Lycoming engines and are probably best remembered for their unusual Gruss air springs whose two vertical cylinders mounted either side of the radiator provided a useful means of recognition. The spring comprised a piston moving up and down against air pressure, its rod being fixed to the front end of a conventional leaf spring. The 168MOT was a variation of the 168OT which had a Meadows engine, in an attempt to increase the power of the model but the engine proved unreliable in service and not many were built. Six, GF 120–125, came to London Transport from Edward Hillman in August 1934. The 166SD and 168SD were normal control versions (SD meaning 'standard drive'), of which totals of 21 and two were acquired. The CP6 (seven acquired) and AS6 (four) were smaller 20-seat normal control one-man buses.

The numbering of the Gilfords was complicated, the main source of the complexity being the practice of London General Country Services not to number their vehicles. This was carried on by the Country Bus department during the eighteen months or so that engineering responsibility remained at Reigate, and Gilfords used as buses had no fleet number until 1935. On the other hand, Green Line Coaches Ltd, although controlled by LGCS, did number its vehicles and the 51 Gilfords acquired before July 1933 became GF 1–51 in its series. All remaining Gilfords which passed into the Country Bus fleet remained unnumbered until 1935 and all but six of the 51 coaches also effectively lost their numbers because they were transferred to bus operation. The six exceptions were GF 22, 23, 25, 26, 28 and 33. The remaining Gilfords acquired as coaches were numbered between 1 and 125 in chronological order of acquisition.

The 168OT was the most common type of Gilford chassis in the LPTB fleet and Wycombe, Gilford's associate company, the most common body make. In the complicated numbering changes carried out on the class, GF 149ʙ had been numbered GF 20 while in use as a coach and was renumbered when it became a bus in 1935. The two cylinders for the Gruss springs are the two vertical projections which look a little like a pair of billycans mounted on each side of the radiator. GF 149ʙ, here in use as a bus at New Barnet, came from the Edward Hillman associate Upminster Services Ltd. D.W.K. Jones

However, when GF 34 and 98 were withdrawn their numbers were taken over by two re-instated coaches formerly numbered GF 27 and 20 respectively Similarly, when GF 65 transferred to bus work in 1935 it was renumbered GF 151 and its original number was taken over by former GF38. These and other similar renumberings are shown in the fleet list. When Country Buses were given fleet numbers from 1935, the Gilfords were numbered in the series GF 126–190, with 191 and 192 being added when the Penn Bus Co. was acquired in August 1935. Twenty-five buses never received fleet numbers. The two Central Bus Gilfords acquired from A.E. Blane of Romford in November 1934 were given the class code GD for reasons unknown. Paradoxically, when three Gilfords were transferred from Country to Central for new route 203 in August 1935, they were numbered in the main series as GF 193–195. To avoid cluttering the text, the suffix letters B and C applied to Country Buses and Green Line coaches respectively have been omitted from the text and list but were carried on the vehicles, as appropriate to their status at any given time (for example: GF 30c and GF 149ʙ).

A large number of GFs was withdrawn during 1934 and 1935 and by the end of June 1936 the number licensed had fallen to 140 (53 Country Buses and 87 Green Line coaches). Most of these were replaced during 1936 by the new 9T9 and 6Q6 coaches and the converted 1/4Q4/1s, leaving one bus and fourteen coaches still at work in June 1937. These were withdrawn and most had been sold out of stock by the end of the year, leaving nine to go during January 1938. Most saw further service with other operators.

This handsome 26-seat Strachan bodied 168OT, GF 160c came from Maidstone & District as a coach and was new in 1930. The metal rainshields over the windows impart a more utilitarian look than the glass fitted to the Wycombes. D.W.K. Jones

The Metcalfe bodies had shallower windows and a slightly higher waistline which upset the proportions of an otherwise well turned out design. As yet unnumbered, this thirty-seater which had been acquired from Sunset Saloon coaches, became GF 87. Behind it at Aldgate is another acquisition from Sunset, still bearing that company's colours. Alan Cross

A fourth body make to be found on 168OT chassis was London Lorries, a popular choice among London coach operators. Numbered GF 106 as a coach, it became GF 139B when transferred to bus work in 1935. It came from Tilbury Coaching Services and was photographed at Hertford bus station alongside Q 65B a mere two years its junior but a world away in modernity of design. J.F. Higham

The nearside of GF 11's Wycombe body shows the curved panel leading into the bulkhead which was a characteristic of this make. New in 1930 to Upminster Services, GF 11 is in bus service parked outside the old Amersham & District garage in May 1935. D.W.K. Jones

GF 123c was one of the rare Meadows engined 168MOT type introduced to increase the power of the model. To house the larger engine, the radiator has been pushed forward to a point between the Gruss cylinders, taking the radiator-mounted headlamps with it. The destination 'Roneo Corner' indicates that the coach has made a garage run to Romford off the Upminster coach route. D.W.K. Jones

The 166OT was a shorter wheelbase version of the 168OT and was less numerous in London. GF 22, new in 1929 to Regent Motor Service of Hornsey and acquired by Green Line Coaches Ltd before the Board was formed, had a Duple body. The style was similar to those found on Premier Line's Tigers in the TR class but the driver's cab and front dash had something of an antique look about them. Alan Cross

Only a year separates the Strachan body on GF 167B, a 166OT, from that of GF 160 (see page 18) but the shallower roof, cruder window finishings, prominent beading and the ornamental bracket in the front canopy all spell an earlier generation. This came from Strawhatter and is at work from Two Waters garage at Boxmoor station. D.W.K. Jones

Yet another variety of Strachan body with cut-away canopy and a lower level for the cab roof, dating from 1929, was carried by GF 169B a 166OT acquired from Peoples of Ware but now operating from Two Waters garage where it is seen parked after finishing work on route 301. D.W.K. Jones

This Wycombe bodied 166OT was a late acquisition from the Penn Bus Co and was still in Penn colours though carrying a LONDON TRANSPORT fleet name when photographed at High Wycombe. J.F. Higham/The Omnibus Society

The Gilford CP6 was a small 20-seat normal control model, seven of which were acquired by London Transport. Strachan bodied VX1541, which came from Eastern National, never received a number. D.W.K. Jones

Wycombe bodied Gilford 166SD GC6350 was given the number GF 29 by Green Line when it was acquired from Associated Coaches (Ongar) Ltd in March 1932 but it did not receive a London Transport number. It was originally a 26-seat coach but had been relegated to bus work by the time of this photograph taken in Slough. J.F. Higham

Thurgood of Ware supplied this neat and workmanlike bus body for GF 171B, which was bought by Peoples Motor Services in 1929. It was still working on a former Peoples route from Hertford garage when photographed in Hertford bus station. C.F. Klapper

Only five of the longer wheelbase 168SD came into the LPTB fleet, all originally owned by the Skylark Motor Coach Co. When the company was taken over by Green Line in February 1932 the Duple body on GF 129B, GF 18 in the Green Line numbering, was a two-door coach but when it was transferred to bus work, London Transport gave it this open front entrance. D.W.K. Jones

The AS6 was the replacement for the CP6 as Gilford's small one-man bus, although the impressive new radiator introduced with this model gave it the appearance of a bigger bus. Strachan bodied GF 194 was one of only three of the class ever to be worked by Central Buses, although there were two GD class Gilford's which did so. GF 194 had operated without a number until transferred to Central Buses in August 1935 for operation on new route 203 to Mitchley Avenue, Purley, at which terminus it is seen here. J.F. Higham

Chassis:	Gilford 166OT (GF 1–3, 22, 23, 25, 33, 65 (UV74), 98 (UR4726), 141, 147, 148, 152, 153, 156–158, 161, 164, 165, 167–169, 173–176, 192, GU2082, KP1487, KX2595, UC3483);		

Chassis: Gilford 166OT (GF 1–3, 22, 23, 25, 33, 65 (UV74), 98 (UR4726), 141, 147, 148, 152, 153, 156–158, 161, 164, 165, 167–169, 173–176, 192, GU2082, KP1487, KX2595, UC3483);
166SD (GF 130–137, 145, 170, 171, 193, 195, GC6350, GC6351, MT1954, MT4600, UR2401, XV7711–7713);
168OT (4–21, 24, 26–32, 34 (both), 35–64, 65 (JD1218), 66–97, 98 (MJ2153), 99–119, 146, 148, 152, 153, 159, 160, 162, 163, 166, 172, 177–187, 190, 191; GD 1–2; KX4984)
168MOT (GF 120–125)
168SD (GF 127–129, 138, 142); CP6 (GC9054, 9055, UP3137, VX1541, 1542, 1560, 1561)
AS6 (GF 194, HX1855, JH2468, KR6744, KX7164)
The following numbers are omitted from the above list as they were the second to be carried by the same vehicle: GF 126, 139, 140, 143, 144, 149–151, 154, 155, 188, 189 (for details of the renumberings see main list).

Engine: Lycoming 6-cylinder 5.8 litre 36hp side valve petrol (166OT, 166SD, 168OT, 168SD)
Buda 6-cylinder 4.55 litre 31.5 hp side valve petrol (CP6, AS6);
Meadows 6-cylinder 115bhp ohv petrol (168MOT)

Transmission: 4-speed crash

Bodywork: Beadle (GF 1); Duple (GF 2, 22, 127–138, 142, 190, 193, GC9054, 9055, JH2468, MT1954, 4600, UP3137, XV7711–7713): London Lorries (GF 26, 28, 34 (UR5888). 103–106; Metcalfe (GF 77–88); Petty (GF 98 (UR4726), 146, 173–187, HX1855, KX7164; Strachan (GF 89–97, 98, 159–163, (MJ2153), 99–101, 167–169, 194, KR6744, KX2595, KX4984, VX1541, 1542, 1560, 1561, ABH366; Thurgood (GF 170, 171, 195, UR2401); Wilton (GF 164);
Wycombe (GF 3–21, 23–25, 27, 29–33, 34(JD611), 35–64, 65 (JD1218), 66–76), 102, 107–125, 141, 145, 147, 148, 152, 153, 156–158, 172, 191, 192, GC6350, 6351, GU2082, KP1487).
The make of bodywork for the following is not known: GF 65 (UV74), 165, 166, UC3483

Capacity: B20F (GF 194, JH2468, KR6744, KX7164, UP3137, VX1541, 1542, 1560, 1561)
B20D (HX1855); B26F (GF148, 195, UR2401); B32F (GF 161, 162, 169–171, 186, 187, 192)
C20F (GC9054, 9055); C26F (GF 4–21[1, 2], 24, 26–64[2], 65 (JD1218), 66–73[1,2], 113–125[1,2], 141, 142, 145, 147, 148, 153, 156–160, 190, GC6350, 6351);
C26? (UC3483)
C26D (127–138, 193, MT1954, 4600, XV7711–7713); C27F (GF 104);
C28F (GF 1); C28D (GF 23, 164); C29F (GF 25, 172,); C30F (GF 65 (UV74), 78–81, 84–88, 100–101[3], 105, 107–112[3], 152); C30R (KX2595, 4984);
C30C (GF 89–97, 98 (MJ2153), 99, 163); C30D (GF 182)
C31F (GF 3, 74–76, 102[4], 146, 165, 166, 173, 174, 177–181, 183–185);
C32F (GF 2, 22, 77, 82, 83, 98 (UR4726), 103, 106, 168, 175, 176, 191);
C32R (GF 167); C32D (GU2082)

L.T. type codes: Not allocated
Built: 1928–1933
Number acquired: 220
Number in stock 1.7.33: 58   31.12.39: Nil   Last out of stock: 15.1.38

The following vehicles had their seating capacity reduced as shown:

1   to 24: GF 6, 68 and 69 (2.36), GF 70 and 71 (3.36), GF 72, 73 and 113 (1.36), GF 116 (9.36)
2   to 25: GF 13 (12.35), GF 15 and 114 (1.36), GF 19 (3.36), GF 26 (date unknown), GF 32 and 118 (10.36), GF 68 (1.35), GF 70 and 115 (11.35)
3   to 29: GF 101 (11.35), 107 (1.36), 108 (2.36), 109 (3.36), 110 (1.37)
4   to 30: GF 102 (10.36)

Final no.	Green Line no.	Acquired from	Date New	Date into stock	Date out of stock
1	EV445	J.H. Price (Super Service Coaches) East Ham	1931	1.12.33	23.4.36
2	UW8810	J.H. Price (Super Service Coaches) East Ham	1929	1.12.33	16.4.36
r 3	UW8811	J.H. Price (Super Service Coaches) East Ham	1929	1.12.33	r
4	JD13	Edward Hillman's Saloon Coaches Ltd, Romford	1929	10.1.34	26.8.36

5	JD14		Edward Hillman's Saloon Coaches Ltd, Romford	1929	10.1.34	22.12.37
6	JD15		Upminster Services Ltd, Romford	1929	10.1.34	14.12.37
7	JD16		Upminster Services Ltd, Romford	1930	10.1.34	15.12.37
8	JD17		Upminster Services Ltd, Romford	1930	10.1.34	1.9.36
9	JD18		Upminster Services Ltd, Romford	1930	10.1.34	19.9.36
10	JD19		Upminster Services Ltd, Romford	1930	10.1.34	13.12.37
11	JD20		Upminster Services Ltd, Romford	1930	10.1.34	1.9.36
12	JD21		Upminster Services Ltd, Romford	1930	10.1.34	13.12.37
13	JD22		Upminster Services Ltd, Romford	1930	10.1.34	14.12.37
14	JD23		Upminster Services Ltd, Romford	1930	10.1.34	3.9.36
15	JD385		Upminster Services Ltd, Romford	1930	10.1.34	13.12.37
16	JD390		Upminster Services Ltd, Romford	1930	10.1.34	13.12.37
17	JD391		Upminster Services Ltd, Romford	1930	10.1.34	7.9.36
18	JD392		Upminster Services Ltd, Romford	1930	10.1.34	9.12.37
19	JD393		Upminster Services Ltd, Romford	1930	10.1.34	14.12.37
r 20	JD394		Upminster Services Ltd, Romford	1930	10.1.34	r
r 21	JD395		Upminster Services Ltd, Romford	1930	10.1.34	r
22	VN535	GF 22	LGCS Ltd (formerly Regent Motor Service, Hornsey)	1929	1.7.33	9.4.36
23	UW1276	GF 23	LGCS Ltd (formerly Regent Motor Service, Hornsey)	1929	1.7.33	17.12.37
24	JD396		Upminster Services Ltd, Romford	1930	10.1.34	9.12.37
25	UR 4879	GF 25	LGCS Ltd (formerly Bucks Expresses (Watford) Ltd)	1929	1.7.33	25.8.36
26	UR5887	GF 26	LGCS Ltd (formerly Bucks Expresses (Watford) Ltd)	1930	1.7.33	31.8.36
27	JD397		Upminster Services Ltd, Romford	1930	10.1.34	21.12.37
28	UR5889	GF 28	LGCS Ltd (formerly Bucks Expresses (Watford) Ltd)	1930	1.7.33	31.8.36
29	JD500		Upminster Services Ltd, Romford	1930	10.1.34	11.12.37
30	JD608		Upminster Services Ltd, Romford	1930	10.1.34	13.12.37
31	JD609		Upminster Services Ltd, Romford	1930	10.1.34	13.12.37
32	JD610		Upminster Services Ltd, Romford	1930	10.1.34	15.1.38
33	GJ1189	GF 33	LGCS Ltd (formerly Associated Coaches (Ongar) Ltd	1930	1.7.33	20.12.37
r1 34	JD611		Upminster Services Ltd, Romford	1930	10.1.34	14.4.36
r1 34	UR5888	GF 27	LGCS Ltd (formerly Bucks Expresses (Watford) Ltd)	1930	1.7.33	25.8.36
35	JD612		Upminster Services Ltd, Romford	1930	10.1.34	23.9.36
36	JD613		Edward Hillman's Saloon Coaches Ltd, Romford	1930	10.1.34	13.12.37
37	JD614		Edward Hillman's Saloon Coaches Ltd, Romford	1930	10.1.34	3.9.36
38	JD615		Edward Hillman's Saloon Coaches Ltd, Romford	1930	10.1.34	29.8.36
39	JD616		Edward Hillman's Saloon Coaches Ltd, Romford	1930	10.1.34	8.35
40	JD687		Edward Hillman's Saloon Coaches Ltd, Romford	1930	10.1.34	15.12.37
41	JD688		Edward Hillman's Saloon Coaches Ltd, Romford	1930	10.1.34	20.12.37
42	JD783		Edward Hillman's Saloon Coaches Ltd, Romford	1930	10.1.34	15.12.37
43	JD784		Edward Hillman's Saloon Coaches Ltd, Romford	1930	10.1.34	25.8.36
44	JD785		Edward Hillman's Saloon Coaches Ltd, Romford	1930	10.1.34	21.12.37
45	JD786		Edward Hillman's Saloon Coaches Ltd, Romford	1930	10.1.34	20.12.37
46	JD1005		Edward Hillman's Saloon Coaches Ltd, Romford	1930	10.1.34	21.12.37
47	JD1006		Edward Hillman's Saloon Coaches Ltd, Romford	1930	10.1.34	11.12.37
48	JD1007		Edward Hillman's Saloon Coaches Ltd, Romford	1930	10.1.34	22.12.37
49	JD1008		Edward Hillman's Saloon Coaches Ltd, Romford	1930	10.1.34	21.12.37
50	JD1009		Edward Hillman's Saloon Coaches Ltd, Romford	1930	10.1.34	21.12.37
51	JD1010		Edward Hillman's Saloon Coaches Ltd, Romford	1930	10.1.34	29.8.36
52	JD1193		Edward Hillman's Saloon Coaches Ltd, Romford	1931	10.1.34	23.12.37
53	JD1194		Edward Hillman's Saloon Coaches Ltd, Romford	1931	10.1.34	26.8.36
54	JD1195		Edward Hillman's Saloon Coaches Ltd, Romford	1931	10.1.34	21.12.37
55	JD1196		Edward Hillman's Saloon Coaches Ltd, Romford	1931	10.1.34	4.9.36
56	JD1197		Edward Hillman's Saloon Coaches Ltd, Romford	1931	10.1.34	17.12.37
57	JD1198		Edward Hillman's Saloon Coaches Ltd, Romford	1931	10.1.34	17.12.37
58	JD1199		Edward Hillman's Saloon Coaches Ltd, Romford	1931	10.1.34	20.12.37
59	JD1200		Edward Hillman's Saloon Coaches Ltd, Romford	1931	10.1.34	9.12.37
60	JD1201		Edward Hillman's Saloon Coaches Ltd, Romford	1931	10.1.34	11.34
61	JD1202		Edward Hillman's Saloon Coaches Ltd, Romford	1931	10.1.34	27.12.37
62	JD1203		Edward Hillman's Saloon Coaches Ltd, Romford	1931	10.1.34	15.12.37
63	JD1204		Edward Hillman's Saloon Coaches Ltd, Romford	1931	10.1.34	21.12.37
64	JD1216		Edward Hillman's Saloon Coaches Ltd, Romford	1931	10.1.34	17.12.37
r2 65	JD1218		Edward Hillman's Saloon Coaches Ltd, Romford	1931	10.1.34	r2
r2 65	UV74	GF 20	LGCS Ltd (formerly Regent Motor Service, Hornsey)	1929	1.7.33	24.12.37
66	JD1219		Edward Hillman's Saloon Coaches Ltd, Romford	1931	10.1.34	21.12.37
67	JD1220		Edward Hillman's Saloon Coaches Ltd, Romford	1931	10.1.34	13.12.37
68	JD1221		Edward Hillman's Saloon Coaches Ltd, Romford	1931	10.1.34	17.12.37
69	JD1222		Upminster Services Ltd, Romford	1931	10.1.34	14.12.37

70	JD1223		Upminster Services Ltd, Romford	1931	10.1.34	20.12.37
71	JD1224		Upminster Services Ltd, Romford	1931	10.1.34	14.12.37
72	JD1225		Upminster Services Ltd, Romford	1931	10.1.34	23.12.37
73	JD1229		Upminster Services Ltd, Romford	1931	10.1.34	15.12.37
r 74	GJ3096		C.E. Holmes (West London Coaches), Maida Hill	1930	17.1.34	r
r 75	GJ5863		C.E. Holmes (West London Coaches), Maida Hill	1930	17.1.34	r
r 76	GJ8862		C.E. Holmes (West London Coaches), Maida Hill	1930	17.1.34	r
77	AEV281		Sunset Pullman Coaches Ltd, Brentwood	1933	25.1.34	22.12.37
78	EV2015		Sunset Pullman Coaches Ltd, Brentwood	1931	25.1.34	15.1.38
79	EV3239		Sunset Pullman Coaches Ltd, Brentwood	1931	25.1.34	10.12.37
80	EV5907		Sunset Pullman Coaches Ltd, Brentwood	1932	25.1.34	23.12.37
81	EV6877		Sunset Pullman Coaches Ltd, Brentwood	1932	25.1.34	15.12.37
82	EV8501		Sunset Pullman Coaches Ltd, Brentwood	1932	25.1.34	22.12.37
83	EV9577		Sunset Pullman Coaches Ltd, Brentwood	1933	25.1.34	23.12.37
84	VX4560		Sunset Pullman Coaches Ltd, Brentwood	1930	25.1.34	23.12.37
85	VX4561		Sunset Pullman Coaches Ltd, Brentwood	1930	25.1.34	15.12.37
86	VX7157		Sunset Pullman Coaches Ltd, Brentwood	1930	25.1.34	17.12.37
87	VX9764		Sunset Pullman Coaches Ltd, Brentwood	1931	25.1.34	14.12.37
88	VX9924		Sunset Pullman Coaches Ltd, Brentwood	1931	25.1.34	23.12.37
89	MJ65		H.E. Hill (Strawhatter Coaches), Luton	1932	1.2.34	15.12.37
90	MJ415		H.E. Hill (Strawhatter Coaches), Luton	1932	1.2.34	18.12.37
91	MJ425		H.E. Hill (Strawhatter Coaches), Luton	1932	1.2.34	21.12.37
92	MJ435		H.E. Hill (Strawhatter Coaches), Luton	1932	1.2.34	15.12.37
93	MJ445		H.E. Hill (Strawhatter Coaches), Luton	1932	1.2.34	30.12.37
94	MJ590		H.E. Hill (Strawhatter Coaches), Luton	1932	1.2.34	15.12.37
95	MJ2150		H.E. Hill (Strawhatter Coaches), Luton	1933	1.2.34	15.12.37
96	MJ2151		H.E. Hill (Strawhatter Coaches), Luton	1933	1.2.34	15.12.37
97	MJ2152		H.E. Hill (Strawhatter Coaches), Luton	1933	1.2.34	24.12.37
r1 98	MJ2153		H.E. Hill (Strawhatter Coaches), Luton	1933	1.2.34	11.34
r1 98	UR4726	GF 38	LGCS Ltd (Acme Pullman Services Ltd, Bishops Stortford)	1929	1.7.33	13.12.37
99	MJ2154		H.E. Hill (Strawhatter Coaches), Luton	1933	1.2.34	15.12.37
100	TM7015		H.E. Hill (Strawhatter Coaches), Luton	1930	1.2.34	15.1.38
101	TM8825		H.E. Hill (Strawhatter Coaches), Luton	1931	1.2.34	22.12.37
102	JD1146		Fleet Transport Services Ltd, Stratford	1931	21.2.34	15.1.38
r 103	EV2507		S.J. & I.M. Skinner (Tilbury Coaching Services)	1931	24.3.34	r
104	VX6352		S.J. & I.M. Skinner (Tilbury Coaching Services)	1930	24.3.34	15.12.37
r 105	VX8858		S.J. & I.M. Skinner (Tilbury Coaching Services)	1930	24.3.34	r
r 106	AHK595		S.J. & I.M. Skinner (Tilbury Coaching Services)	1933	24.3.34	r
107	EV7578		Edward Hillman's Saloon Coaches Ltd, Bow	1932	13.8.34	15.12.37
108	EV8106		Edward Hillman's Saloon Coaches Ltd, Bow	1932	13.8.34	27.12.37
109	EV8107		Edward Hillman's Saloon Coaches Ltd, Bow	1932	13.8.34	6.1.38
110	EV8108		Edward Hillman's Saloon Coaches Ltd, Bow	1932	13.8.34	15.12.37
111	EV8905		Edward Hillman's Saloon Coaches Ltd, Bow	1932	13.8.34	9.12.37
112	EV9018		Edward Hillman's Saloon Coaches Ltd, Bow	1932	13.8.34	14.12.37
113	JD1227		Edward Hillman's Saloon Coaches Ltd, Bow	1931	13.8.34	15.1.38
114	JD1228		Edward Hillman's Saloon Coaches Ltd, Bow	1931	13.8.34	21.12.37
115	JD1552		Edward Hillman's Saloon Coaches Ltd, Bow	1931	13.8.34	10.12.37
116	JD1553		Edward Hillman's Saloon Coaches Ltd, Bow	1931	13.8.34	24.12.37
r 117	JD1555		Edward Hillman's Saloon Coaches Ltd, Bow	1931	13.8.34	r
118	JD1556		Edward Hillman's Saloon Coaches Ltd, Bow	1931	13.8.34	9.12.37
119	JD1557		Edward Hillman's Saloon Coaches Ltd, Bow	1931	13.8.34	17.12.37
120	JD1976		Edward Hillman's Saloon Coaches Ltd, Bow	1932	13.8.34	18.12.37
121	JD1977		Edward Hillman's Saloon Coaches Ltd, Bow	1932	13.8.34	18.12.37
122	JD1978		Edward Hillman's Saloon Coaches Ltd, Bow	1932	13.8.34	6.1.38
123	JD1979		Edward Hillman's Saloon Coaches Ltd, Bow	1932	13.8.34	13.12.37
r 124	JD1980		Edward Hillman's Saloon Coaches Ltd, Bow	1932	13.8.34	r
125	JD1981		Edward Hillman's Saloon Coaches Ltd, Bow	1932	13.8.34	15.12.37
r 126	GJ3096		C.E. Holmes (West London Coaches), Maida Hill	1930	17.1.34	25.8.36
127	HX579	GF 16	LGCS Ltd (formerly Skylark Motor Coach Co Ltd)	1930	1.7.33	3.2.36
128	HX580	GF 17	LGCS Ltd (formerly Skylark Motor Coach Co Ltd)	1930	1.7.33	10.3.36
129	HX1107	GF 18	LGCS Ltd (formerly Skylark Motor Coach Co Ltd)	1930	1.7.33	23.3.36
130	MY346	GF 7	LGCS Ltd (formerly Skylark Motor Coach Co Ltd)	1929	1.7.33	3.2.36
131	MY1240	GF 8	LGCS Ltd (formerly Skylark Motor Coach Co Ltd)	1929	1.7.33	6.2.36
132	MY1241	GF 9	LGCS Ltd (formerly Skylark Motor Coach Co Ltd)	1929	1.7.33	13.2.36
133	MY1914	GF 10	LGCS Ltd (formerly Skylark Motor Coach Co Ltd)	1929	1.7.33	3.2.36
134	MY2004	GF 11	LGCS Ltd (formerly Skylark Motor Coach Co Ltd)	1929	1.7.33	6.3.36

135	MY2005	GF 12	LGCS Ltd (formerly Skylark Motor Coach Co Ltd)	1929	1.7.33	3.2.36
136	MY2006	GF 13	LGCS Ltd (formerly Skylark Motor Coach Co Ltd)	1929	1.7.33	21.3.36
137	MY2290	GF 14	LGCS Ltd (formerly Skylark Motor Coach Co Ltd)	1929	1.7.33	12.2.36
138	MY3462	GF 15	LGCS Ltd (formerly Skylark Motor Coach Co Ltd)	1930	1.7.33	23.3.36
r 139	AHK595		S.J. & I.M. Skinner (Tilbury Coaching Services)	1933	24.3.34	22.12.37
r 140	EV2507		S.J. & I.M. Skinner (Tilbury Coaching Services)	1931	24.3.34	23.12.37
141	GH3119	GF 35	LGCS Ltd (formerly Associated Coaches, Ongar, Ltd)	1930	1.7.33	11.12.37
142	GH9949	GF 50	LGCS Ltd (formerly C.W.B. Lewis (Cream Line Coaches), Potters Bar	1930	1.7.33	2.9.36
r 143	GJ5863		C.E. Holmes (West London Coaches), Maida Hill	1930	17.1.34	11.12.37
r 144	GJ8862		C.E. Holmes (West London Coaches), Maida Hill	1930	17.1.34	22.12.37
145	UR6517		F. Steer (Colne Services), London Colney	1930	1.11.33	18.12.37
146	UR6897	GF 44	LGCS Ltd (Acme Pullman Services Ltd, Bishops Stortford)	1930	1.7.33	13.12.37
147	GJ9121	GF 34	LGCS Ltd (formerly Associated Coaches, Ongar, Ltd)	1930	1.7.33	18.12.37
u 148	JD386		Edward Hillman's Saloon Coaches Ltd, Romford	1930	10.1.34	11.12.37
r 149	JD394		Edward Hillman's Saloon Coaches Ltd, Romford	1930	10.1.34	15.12.37
r 150	JD395		Edward Hillman's Saloon Coaches Ltd, Romford	1930	10.1.34	23.12.37
r2 151	JD1218		Edward Hillman's Saloon Coaches Ltd, Romford	1930	10.1.34	10.12.37
u 152	JD1226		Edward Hillman's Saloon Coaches Ltd, Bow	1931	13.8.34	11.12.37
u 153	JD1554		Edward Hillman's Saloon Coaches Ltd, Bow	1931	13.8.34	21.12.37
154	JD1555		Edward Hillman's Saloon Coaches Ltd, Bow	1931	13.8.34	22.12.37
155	JD1980		Edward Hillman's Saloon Coaches Ltd, Bow	1932	13.8.34	18.12.37
156	KP1484		Maidstone & District Motor Services Ltd	1928	1.7.33	5.9.36
157	KP1485		Maidstone & District Motor Services Ltd	1928	1.7.33	31.7.36
158	KP1486		Maidstone & District Motor Services Ltd	1928	1.7.33	9.4.37
159	KR5571		Maidstone & District Motor Services Ltd	1930	1.7.33	6.1.38
160	KR5572		Maidstone & District Motor Services Ltd	1930	1.7.33	6.1.38
161	KX1923		Amersham & District Motor Bus & Haulage Co Ltd	1929	24.11.33	15.12.37
162	KX3928		Amersham & District Motor Bus & Haulage Co Ltd	1930	24.11.33	10.12.37
163	MJ75		H.E. Hill (Strawhatter Coaches), Luton	1932	1.2.34	22.12.37
164	MT1841	GF 21	LGCS Ltd (formerly Regent Motor Service, Hornsey)	1929	1.7.33	31.8.36
165	MT3619		W.D. Beaumont & A.W. Priest (Beaumont's Safeway Coaches), Enfield	1929	28.4.34	23.12.37
166	MY7213		W.D. Beaumont & A.W. Priest (Beaumont's Safeway Coaches), Enfield	1930	28.3.34	24.12.37
167	TM4495		H.E. Hill (Strawhatter Coaches), Luton	1929	1.2.34	22.12.37
168	TM5329		H.E. Hill (Strawhatter Coaches), Luton	1929	1.2.34	2.9.36
169	UL8972		Peoples Motor Services Ltd, Ware	1929	1.12.33	10.12.37
170	UR3616		F. Steer (Colne Services), London Colney	1929	1.11.33	18.12.37
171	UR3969		Peoples Motor Services Ltd, Ware	1929	1.12.33	15.12.37
172	UR4712	GF 24	LGCS Ltd (formerly Bucks Expresses (Watford) Ltd)	1929	1.7.33	17.12.37
173	UR4915	GF 39	LGCS Ltd (Acme Pullman Services Ltd, Bishops Stortford)	1929	1.7.33	21.12.37
174	UR4916	GF 40	LGCS Ltd (Acme Pullman Services Ltd, Bishops Stortford)	1929	1.7.33	15.12.37
175	UR4724	GF 36	LGCS Ltd (Acme Pullman Services Ltd, Bishops Stortford)	1929	1.7.33	22.12.37
176	UR4725	GF 37	LGCS Ltd (Acme Pullman Services Ltd, Bishops Stortford)	1929	1.7.33	22.12.37
177	UR5158	GF 41	LGCS Ltd (Acme Pullman Services Ltd, Bishops Stortford)	1929	1.7.33	11.12.37
178	UR5641	GF 42	LGCS Ltd (Acme Pullman Services Ltd, Bishops Stortford)	1930	1.7.33	22.12.37
179	UR5642	GF 43	LGCS Ltd (Acme Pullman Services Ltd, Bishops Stortford)	1930	1.7.33	17.12.37
180	UR6898	GF 45	LGCS Ltd (Acme Pullman Services Ltd, Bishops Stortford)	1930	1.7.33	14.12.37
181	UR6899	GF 46	LGCS Ltd (Acme Pullman Services Ltd, Bishops Stortford)	1930	1.7.33	23.12.37
182	UR7311		W.H. Flower & C.H. Etches (City Omnibus Services), St Albans	1930	29.3.34	23.12.37
183	UR7534	GF 47	LGCS Ltd (Acme Pullman Services Ltd, Bishops Stortford)	1930	1.7.33	23.12.37
184	UR7535	GF 48	LGCS Ltd (Acme Pullman Services Ltd, Bishops Stortford)	1930	1.7.33	13.12.37

185	UR7536	GF 49	LGCS Ltd (Acme Pullman Services Ltd, Bishops Stortford)	1930	1.7.33	30.12.37
186	UR7801		W.H. Flower & C.H. Etches (City Omnibus Services), St Albans	1930	29.3.34	24.12.37
187	UR7942		A.P.& P.B. Morgan (Comfy Coaches), Harpenden	1930	6.2.34	18.6.35
r 188	UW8811		J.H. Price (Super Service Coaches), East Ham	1929	1.12.33	18.12.37
189	VX8858		S.J. & I.M. Skinner (Tilbury Coaching Services)	1930	24.3.34	14.12.37
190	YY8349	GF 51	LGCS Ltd (formerly C.W.B. Lewis (Cream Line C'ches)	1932	1.7.33	23.12.37
191	KX7843		The Penn Bus Company Ltd	1931	1.8.35	23.12.37
192	UV7778		The Penn Bus Company Ltd	1929	1.8.35	14.12.37
u1 193	MT1800	GF 4	LGCS Ltd (formerly Skylark Motor Coach Co Ltd)	1929	1.7.33	25.5.36
u1 194	ABH366		Amersham & District Motor Bus & Haulage Co Ltd	1933	24.11.33	20.6.36
u1 195	UR2402		Peoples Motor Services Ltd, Ware	1929	1.12.33	25.5.36

Unnumbered Gilfords

This list does not include vehicles which ran unnumbered for a time and then received numbers

GC6350	GF 29	LGCS Ltd (formerly Associated Coaches, Ongar, Ltd)	1930	1.7.33	15.1.36
GC6351	GF 30	LGCS Ltd (formerly Associated Coaches, Ongar, Ltd)	1930	1.7.33	7.35
GC9054	GF 31	LGCS Ltd (formerly Associated Coaches, Ongar, Ltd)	1929	1.7.33	10.35
GC9055	GF 32	LGCS Ltd (formerly Associated Coaches, Ongar, Ltd)	1929	1.7.33	7.35
GU2082		Sunshine Saloon Coaches Ltd, Kingston	1929	30.12.33	5.34
HX1855		Amersham & District Motor Bus & Haulage Co Ltd	1930	24.11.33	9.35
JH2468		F. Steer (Colne Services), London Colney	1932	1.11.33	11.35
KP1487		Maidstone & District Motor Services Ltd	1928	1.7.33	5.35
KR6744		Maidstone & District Motor Services Ltd	1930	1.7.33	9.1.36
KX2595		Amersham & District Motor Bus & Haulage Co Ltd	1929	24.11.33	10.34
KX4984		Amersham & District Motor Bus & Haulage Co Ltd	1930	24.11.33	10.34
KX7164		Amersham & District Motor Bus & Haulage Co Ltd	1931	24.11.33	12.35
MT1954	GF 5	LGCS Ltd (formerly Skylark Motor Coach Co Ltd)	1929	1.7.33	11.35
MT4600	GF 6	LGCS Ltd (formerly Skylark Motor Coach Co Ltd)	1929	1.7.33	10.35
UC3483		W.H. Flower & C.H. Etches (City Omnibus Services), St Albans	1928	29.3.34	10.34
UP3137		H.G. & F.I. Biggerstaff (Biggerstaff's Bus Ser.) Sarratt	1929	8.11.33	10.35
UR2401		Peoples Motor Services Ltd, Ware	1929	1.12.33	12.35
VX1541		Eastern National Omnibus Co Ltd	1929	1.9.33	10.35
VX1542		Eastern National Omnibus Co Ltd	1929	1.9.33	5.35
VX1560		Eastern National Omnibus Co Ltd	1929	1.9.33	c 12.35
VX1561		Eastern National Omnibus Co Ltd	1929	1.9.33	5.35
XV7711	GF 1	LGCS Ltd (formerly Skylark Motor Coach Co Ltd)	1928	1.7.33	7.35
XV7712	GF 2	LGCS Ltd (formerly Skylark Motor Coach Co Ltd)	1928	1.7.33	6.2.36
XV7713	GF 3	LGCS Ltd (formerly Skylark Motor Coach Co Ltd)	1928	1.7.33	13.2.36

GD CLASS Gilford 168OT Metcalfe B26F (Central Bus acquisitions)

1	TR8755	A.E. Blane Ltd (Imperial Bus Services), Romford	1930	28.11.34	18.6.35
2	TR8754	A.E. Blane Ltd (Imperial Bus Services), Romford	1930	28.11.34	c 18.6.35

c   Chassis only body scrapped earlier
r   GF 3, 20, 21, 74–76, 103, 105, 106, 117, 124 renumbered GF 188, 149, 150, 126, 143, 144, 140, 189, 139, 154, 155 as buses in 1935
r1   Ex-Hillman GF 34 and ex-LGCS GF 98 were withdrawn from service in 1934 some time after which former Green Line GF 27 and 38 were reinstated as coaches as GF 34 and 98 respectively
r2   Ex-Hillman GF 65 (JD1218) renumbered GF 151 as a bus in 1935; the number GF 65 was then allocated to former Green Line GF 27
u   Ran unnumbered as a coach for a time before receiving this number as a country bus
u1   Ran unnumbered as country buses until transferred to Central Buses 22.8.35.

R

The Reliance was a modified version of the ADC 426 chassis which was introduced by the Associated Equipment Company Ltd in 1929 to bridge the gap until the new Regal, Regent and Renown models could go into production. The important new element was the Rackham-designed 6-cylinder engine, a 6.1 litre unit classified A130 by AEC, which replaced the 4-cylinder designs of earlier models. One of the three prototypes rebuilt from ADC 426 chassis was delivered to East Surrey in November 1928 and is believed to have been the first to go into service (PK 4243) but there is no trace of the fate of this bus after the formation of LGCS in 1932. The LGOC purchased a total of 34 for delivery in 1929, of which fourteen were 29-seat buses (R 26–34, 45–49 in the LPTB numbering, originally R 6–14, 1–5) and 20 were 31-seat coaches (LPTB R 6–25) all with LGOC-built rear-entrance bodywork. A further five were added to the fleet in 1930 (LPTB R 1–5) but these received second-hand 28-seat coach bodies which had been transferred from ADCs operated by National. Another nine similar coach bodies were transferred from ADCs to a like number of existing Reliances (LPTB R 26–34), in exchange for their bus bodies. The coaches, whose bodies were described as 'semi-saloons', were originally for Private Hire work and their roofs had a central canvas section which could be folded back. Twenty were later used on Green Line coach services for which they were fitted with standard destination indicator boxes. R 44 was an oddity, being an open-top double-decker which was bought by East Surrey in 1928. It did not receive its number until 1935.

These five single-deck buses, one double-decker and 34 coaches joined the Country Bus & Coach fleet when the LPTB was formed and, apart from four which were sold in 1934, remained there until withdrawn in 1938. Nine more coaches were acquired with the Battens undertaking in December 1933 (R 35–43) and also joined the Country fleet, being used indiscriminately as buses or coaches.

Thirty-one of the Reliances were given new Weymann metal-framed 30-seat front entrance bus bodies in 1935, including R 44 which then became a standard single-deck bus. The body from R 44 was transferred to R 40 in August 1937 and its chassis was scrapped. The Weymann bodies were transferred to renovated T-type chassis in 1938 and the Reliance chassis scrapped. The remaining vehicles which had not been rebodied were also withdrawn during 1938.

The LGOC coach body fitted to R 32 was its second, having been transferred from a National ADC in exchange for its original bus body. It is about to be removed to make way for its third, a new Weymann metal-framed model, which it received in 1935. This type of body was known as 'semi-saloon' in recognition of the fact that the centre of the roof could be rolled back in good weather.
Ken Glazier collection

Battens of East Ham, who had operated an Aldgate to Tilbury service, handed over nine AEC Reliances to London Transport. R 37c had a well-proportioned Clark 27-seat body, one of the three different makes represented in the small fleet. It has been fitted with a full-size indicator box at the front and standard Green Line side boards, which indicate that it is apparently on layover at Brixton Hill Private Hire garage between spells of duty on the C routes. Ken Glazier collection

Ex-Battens R 39c has a Park Royal body with shallower windows and a higher waist than the Clark example and also lacks a driver's cab door. It is in use as a bus at Hemel Hempstead but still carries the first style of Green Line fleet name used by London Transport. The Reliance had introduced the famous AEC blue triangle when it was launched in 1929 but this was attached to an ADC style radiator shell, the full transformation having to wait for the new generation of chassis launched later the same year. Ken Glazier collection

Chassis:	AEC Reliance 660							
Engine:	AEC A130 6-cylinder 6.1 litre 95 bhp petrol							
Transmission:	AEC 4-speed spur gear							

Chassis: AEC Reliance 660
Engine: AEC A130 6-cylinder 6.1 litre 95 bhp petrol
Transmission: AEC 4-speed spur gear
Bodywork: LGOC (R 1–34*, 44*, 45–49); Clark (R 37, 38); Hall Lewis (R 35): Park Royal (R 36, 39, 43); Short Bros. (R 40, 41, 42)
Capacity: B29R (R 45–49); C26F (R 38); C27F (R 37); C28R (R 1–5, 26–34*); C30R (R 40); C30F (R 35, 36, 39, 43); C31R (R 6–25*); C32R (R 41); C 31R (R 6–25*, 42); O22/24R (R44*)
Built: 1928 (R 44); 1929 (R 6–34, 37, 45–49); 1930 (R 1–5, 38, 40–42); 1931 (R 35, 36, 39, 43)
Number acquired: 49
Number in stock: 1.7.33: 40   31.12.39: Nil
  * R1–16, 19, 20, 22–24, 26–34, 44 were fitted with new Weymann B30F bodies in 1935

All acquired from LGCS on 1.7.33 unless otherwise shown.

R		Date into stock	Date out of stock	R		Date into stock	Date out of stock
1	GF495		6.1.39	26	YW8049		5.1.39
2	GF496		29.11.38	27	UU6601		5.1.39
3	GF497		4.1.39	28	UU6602		5.1.39
4	GF498		5.10.38	29	UU6603		6.1.39
5	GF499		29.11.38	30	UU6604		4.1.39
6	YW8015		29.11.38	31	UU6605		30.11.38
7	YW8016		5.1.39	32	UU6606		30.11.38
8	YW8017		5.1.39	33	UU6607		4.1.39
9	YW8018		9.1.39	34	UU6608		9.1.39
10	YW8019		6.1.39	* 35	HV1136	22.12.33	21.7.38
11	YW8020		4.1.39	* 36	HV1138	22.12.33	21.7.38
12	YW8021		30.11.38	* 37	HM9836	22.12.33	18.7.38
13	YW8024		5.1.39	* 38	HV727	22.12.33	10.6.38
14	YW8025		6.1.39	* 39	HV1393	22.12.33	18.7.38
15	YW8027		30.11.38	* 40	KR5132	22.12.33	9.1.39
16	YW8028		5.10.38	* 41	HV62	22.12.33	6.5.38
17	YW8029		3.34	* 42	HV66	22.12.33	15.7.38
18	YW8030		3.34	* 43	HV1137	22.12.33	13.7.38
19	YW8031		6.1.39	44	UC2265		c 14.10.37
20	YW8032		5.1.39	45	YW8044		15.7.38
21	YW8035		3.34	46	YW8045		6.9.38
22	YW8036		4.1.39	47	YW8046		6.9.38
23	YW8037		3.34	48	YW8047		6.9.38
24	YW8038		5.1.39	49	YW8048		6.9.38
25	YW8039		4.34				

* R 35–43 were acquired with the business of The Amalgamated Omnibus Service and Supplies Ltd (Battens)
c Chassis only; body transferred to R 40

The 30-seat Weymann metal-framed bodies fitted to 31 Reliances in 1935 were a handsome modern design which sat uncomfortably with the antiquated looking radiator. R 14B demonstrates this dissonance at Hemel Hempstead during its three year life in this condition. This body was transferred to T 276 in 1938.
The Omnibus Society

The five 1T1s which had been assigned to East Surrey in 1931 kept their open rear entrances and had some detailed changes made during their five years of freedom from Chiswick's direct influence. T 35 at Nazeing in 1937 has lost the deep moulding below its saloon windows and the glass rainshields which once sat above the opening windows and has acquired a continuous metal rainshield along the length of the saloon and a thick beading above the skirt panels. T 35 was withdrawn in 1939. A.W. Monk

T

The T class, based on the AEC Regal 662 chassis, was first introduced as a bus by the London General Omnibus Company in 1929, when the first of fifty twenty-six foot long 30-seaters were put into service (T 1–37, 39–50, 156; classified 1T1, with variations, when codes were introduced in 1934). As required by contemporary Metropolitan Police regulations, they had doorless rear entrances but were fitted with enclosed drivers' cabs and glass windscreens from the outset. T 43 differed from the rest in having one of five experimental eight-cylinder in-line engines, the others being fitted to ST and LT class double-deckers. To reconcile the greater length of the engine, the radiator was moved forward by about six inches and the bonnet extended. The limit of twenty-six feet on the maximum length of the vehicle was honoured by shortening the fifth bay, above the rear wheel arch. The engine was replaced by a standard six-cylinder unit in December 1930 and its body exchanged with that from T 10. The shortened body remained on T 10 for the rest of its life but the bus was inaccurately classified 1T1, while the now standard T 43 became a 2T2. Five of the type were transferred to the East Surrey Traction Company in 1931 and became part of the London Transport Country Bus fleet in 1933 (T 15, 21, 25, 26 and 35; coded 5/1T1/1 in 1933). The 1T1s which were not transferred to East Surrey were rebuilt with front entrances between May 1933 and March 1935.

T 156 was a replacement for T 38 whose chassis was diverted to become a prototype coach for the newly developing suburban coach services (later Green Line). Like the buses, T 38 was of six-bay construction but the internal floor level was much higher so that all twenty-eight seats could face forward. The entrance was behind the rear wheels and was enclosed by a swing door. This arrangement required an emergency exit, which was another hinged door in the centre of the rear wall.

The next 150 Regals were twenty-seven seat coaches which differed in a number of respects from T 38 (T 51–149, 155, 157–206; 7T7). They had seven-bay rather than six-bay bodywork, a more rounded back and roof and a recessed swing door which reduced the seating capacity by one. On these the emergency door was moved to the first bay on the offside. The body contracts for these were shared between the LGOC, Hall Lewis (the predecessor of Park Royal) and Short Bros. of Rochester. A further hundred coaches (T 207–306) were of broadly similar design but were thirty-seaters, had shallower roofs, a neater indicator box, a rear emergency door and the entrance at the front, enclosed by a sliding door. The bodywork was supplied by Duple, Ransomes Sims and Jefferies and Weymann. All but three of the coach Regals had the standard mechanical specification with petrol engines but T 216, 274 and 305 were fitted with AEC Acro oil engines when new. As with other Acro engines, these were modified later to the Ricardo design. T 268 had been destroyed in an accident in February 1932, but the remaining 249 coaches passed to London Transport.

The 7T7s and 1/7T7/1s remained in Green Line service until 1938 when they were replaced by the new 10T10s. Forty-one 7T7s remained in stock at the end of 1939, two having been converted to lorries and the remainder sold to dealers. Only eight 1/7T7/1s had been sold out of stock. Twenty-six had been used in the programme of conversion to 11T11 (see below), twenty-three had been converted to Service Vehicles, two dismantled and sixteen were put in store. The remaining twenty-four were transferred to bus work, the only significant alteration to their bodies being the installation of a standard size destination indicator box at the front.

The 7T7s were the first purpose-built Green Line coaches and had 27 seats, a rear entrance and an offside emergency exit door. T 101 is at Watford working on route I, the new letter adopted under the post-Amulree changes in October 1933, and has yet to have the London Transport name added to its side panels. J.F. Higham

The canvas roof of Hoyal-bodied T 151 has been rolled back, so demonstrating the extent to which the coach could be opened up to the summer sun while at work on private hire duties. The 8T8s were 27-feet long and seated 32, the normal limit of 26-feet, which applied in the Metropolis when they were built, being avoided because they were not used on stage carriage duties.
J.F. Higham

T 150–154 (8T8) were private hire coaches originally supplied to East Surrey and as they were not intended for stage carriage work, the regulations allowed them to be twenty-seven feet long. Their thirty-two seat bodies, which were built by Hoyal of Weybridge, had folding roofs and swing doors. They remained part of the London Transport private hire fleet until 1938, when they were replaced by the LTC class.

Although the business of Thomas Tilling Ltd was not acquired until 1st October 1933, the twelve AEC Regals operated on behalf of the LGOC since 1932 passed into London Transport ownership on 1st July 1933. They were then formally placed on loan to Tilling. T 307–318 (3T3) had Tilling's own distinctive style of twenty-eight seat front entrance bodywork (later increased to thirty), based on their contemporary double-deck STL design, with a wider and shallower destination blind box than the LGOC version. T 307 and 308 had D128 Daimler preselective gearboxes when new but these were replaced by standard D124 crash boxes, as carried by the remainder, in May and September 1934 respectively, the D128 boxes being installed in double-deck LTs. These buses were used on route 109 (renumbered 227 in 1934) but London Transport replaced them at Bromley by the larger LT and transferred them to Kingston garage.

To enable a sliding door to be installed at the front of the saloon, the 1/7T7/1 type had an offside rather than a nearside fuel tank, which helped to tidy up the appearance from this point of view. In the early days of its operation by the LPTB, T 220 has been turned out freshly painted for use on post-Amulree route BM, Reigate's aversion to vehicle identities being evident in the overpainting of the metal fleet number on the bonnet side.
Snook & Son; Ken Glazier collection

There was no fundamental difference in design between the first two batches of Green Line T but the removal of the emergency door from the offside to the back wall of the body and the better integrated destination indicator box, gave the 1/7T7/1 a neater and sleeker finish. T 218c is at Windsor bus station wearing the first London Transport style of livery used until 1936, with 'GREEN LINE' on the waist panel and cab dash and 'LONDON TRANSPORT' on the main side panels. J.F. Higham

The original body of T 232c was destroyed in an accident in April 1933 and Weymann supplied this 35-seat replacement, which was of Metro-Cammell patented all-metal construction and nine inches longer. It was unique in the fleet and the use of blinds rather than sideboards was never taken up then or at any future time by London Transport or its successors. D.W.K. Jones

The 3T3 former Tilling Regals had the same distinctive body styling as their double-deck contemporaries and a wider indicator box than others in the class, originally with a separate route number. All were replaced at Bromley by single-deck LTs and were sent to Kingston, where T 316 was allocated when photographed at Staines on route 218.
D.W.K. Jones

The Tillings had always carried the numbers T 307–318 but these were duplicated by Green Line Coaches Ltd who allocated their own numbers independently of Chiswick after 1932. The numbers T 307, 308 and 346–358 were allocated to AEC Regal coaches acquired with the businesses of Independent operators taken over in 1932 and 1933. T 307 and 308 were from Bucks Expresses and had Dodson bodywork similar to the 1/7T7/1s. T 346–351 (5T4) were from Blue Belle and had 26ft long London Lorries bodies with rear swing doors. T 352–357 (6T5) were from Queen Line, and had improved specification London Lorries thirty-one-seat bodies with sliding rear doors. T 358 (1/8T8/4) came from Aston of Watford and had a thirty-seat rear entrance body with sliding door, by Strachan. Of the intervening numbers, T 309–324 were built as private hire coaches for East Surrey but later passed to Green Line. All had Hall Lewis bodywork, T 309–314 (8T8/2) being 27ft long twenty-nine seaters with sliding roof, no nearside canopy and two swing-type passenger doors. T 315–324 had the improved 1931 chassis specification with triple servo brakes, and twenty-nine seat front entrance bodies with full-width canopies and all-weather folding roofs (8T8/1). The numbers T 325–345 were assigned to twenty-one coaches owned by Autocar but these passed to Maidstone & District, not London Transport and the numbers were never used. When the responsibility for Country Bus engineering passed to Chiswick in 1935 it was found that the numbers of T 307–318 clashed with those allocated to the Tilling buses and they were renumbered as T 391–402.

T 346–357 were withdrawn from Green Line work in 1935, brought up to standard specification with triple servo brakes and had their coach bodies replaced by new front entrance bus bodies by Weymann similar to those mounted on the Reliance chassis. At first they had only twenty-six seats and these were of the tubular framed variety, rather than the wood-framed type used on the R class. They were reclassified 5T4. The seating was increased to thirty on T 356 in February 1938 and on the rest between January and April 1939. T 319–324 and 391–402 continued as private hire coaches until being replaced by the LTC class between October 1937 and June 1938. T 396 had been withdrawn in January 1938 and was the prototype conversion for the 11T11 class. T 391 and 392 became buses on the arrival of the 10T10s in 1938.

T 351 as taken over from Blue Belle Coaches with the London Lorries 31-seat rear entrance body it carried until 1935. These bodies were quite rakish looking, with a touch of additional style given by the windows being radiused, and had shallower roofs and windows than the LGOC designs. J.F. Higham

T 351 with the new Weymann body it received in 1935, identical to those attached to Reliance chassis in the same year except in having tubular framed seats, but making happier congress with the more modern looking Regal radiator. Unlike the 11T11 conversions of 1938 which appeared to be identical, these twelve vehicles retained their petrol engines and were classified 5T4. Although clearly buses, the 5T4s were dressed as coaches and used in that role for some time. J.F. Higham

This stylish 31-seat coach had a Harrington body, a make not usually associated with London Transport, and came from the fleet of the Lewis Omnibus Company of Watford. T 363 is on Private Hire duty and has its sliding roof open, throwing light onto the individual curved-back seats. D.W.K. Jones

The LPTB also acquired ten Regal coaches directly from Independent operators. T 359, 361, 362 and 364–366 (1/8T8/3) came from the Amersham & District Motor Bus and Haulage Co. and T 360, 363, 367 and 368 (1/8T8/3) from the Lewis Omnibus Co. Ltd of Watford. The Amersham & District vehicles all had 27ft long Strachan rear entrance bodywork with sliding doors, while those from Lewis, also 27ft long, had Harrington bodies. T 360 and 363 were thirty-one seaters with folding roof, two swing passenger doors and no nearside canopy. T 367 and 368, which went into the private hire fleet, were thirty-two seaters with sliding roofs, full-width canopies and sliding passenger doors. T 359, 361, 362 and 364–366 joined the Green Line fleet where they remained until withdrawn in 1938. The others were designed for long distance and private hire work and were therefore allocated to the private hire department until being replaced in 1938. T 359, 361, 362 and 364 were converted to 11T11s in 1938, while similar treatment had been intended for T 365–367 but after an initial conversion these three were converted back and withdrawn.

Three buses were acquired from Independents, T 369 and 371 from the Watford Omnibus Co. and T 370 from Charles Russett and Son (St Albans and District). They were coded 4/1T6. T 369 had an LGOC body fitted when it was sent to Peru as a demonstrator in 1930 but had been acquired by the Watford company in 1932 who had the platform reversed. T 371, another former demonstrator had a thirty-seat front entrance body, possibly by Short Bros. T 370 had been fitted with a second-hand rear entrance body by Short Bros. when purchased by Russett. T 370 received a second-hand Tilling thirty seat front-entrance body in September 1936, becoming 4/1T3 and T 369 a second-hand T7/1 body in April 1938, making it a 1/7T7/1. Only T 369 remained in service at the end of 1939.

Hall Lewis, the predecessor of Park Royal, were the builders of the 30-seat bus body carried by T 371B, one of a pair taken from the Watford Omnibus Company in whose service they were painted pale blue. The company was taken over by LGCS on the very day that the LPTB was formed. T 371B is outside the Astoria cinema in Chesham, an important source of evening traffic for local bus services in the 1930s. J.F. Higham

T 372–379 and 383–390 (4/1T6) were originally East Surrey buses and had Hall Lewis bodies similar to the 1T1 class. T 380–382, also East Surrey buses, had 27ft long Weymann front-entrance bodies of LGOC design but with rounded cabs and emergency exits at the rear. All were delicensed in 1938/1939, being replaced by other vehicles displaced by the arrival of the 10T10s, and fourteen had been sold or scrapped by the end of 1939. The other eight were in store.

The East Surrey Traction Company, the antecedent of LGCS, had sixteen of these Hall Lewis-bodied rear-entrance 30-seaters which were identical to the 1T1 type in its original form. There were also three with forward-entrances and rounded cab which were two years younger (T 380–382). Fresh out of the paint shop, T 378B is at Uxbridge on a former Amersham & District route, by now numbered 455. The Omnibus Society

The Dodson body which came with T 392c when Green Line acquired Bucks Expresses in 1932, was very similar to the 1/7T7/1 design but had higher windows, deeper side panels and a smoother front dome. It is in Golders Green station forecourt on the unique rail-feeder Green Line route T from Watford. J.F. Higham

Green Line, unaware of the existence of the Tilling Ts, used the same numbers for two acquired vehicles and ten of the fifteen touring coaches taken over from East Surrey. T 309, photographed for the record in its new LPTB trim, was one of the latter and was later renumbered T 393. The 29-seat 27ft long body was a Hall Lewis product and the coach was new in 1930. Note the legal lettering giving the Reigate address of the Country Bus department and the formal designation of the rear door as the emergency exit. London's Transport Museum

For buses surviving a failed experiment, the CB type Ts had a remarkably long operational life, not being withdrawn until February 1938. Although they had bodywork similar to the 1T1s, their Chiswick-designed elongated bonnets and unusual radiators ensured instantaneous recognition. They were allocated to Weybridge garage and were normally found on route 219, which at the time of the photograph still continued beyond Weybridge to Woking. Ken Glazier collection

There were three other vehicles inherited from the LGOC which were not AEC Regals but were included in the class by the LGOC for convenience (T 1000–1002; classified CB). These had experimental chassis built by the LGOC in 1931, part of an aborted project which was also intended to encompass vehicles similar to the ST and LT classes but, apart from the Ts, extended only to four LTs. As built, they had six-cylinder Meadows petrol engines but these were replaced with AEC engines between December 1932 and November 1933. They had shortened versions of the contemporary single-deck LT body, T 1001 having no rear destination box. All three were withdrawn in February 1938 and remained in store awaiting sale at the end of 1939.

In 1938, when the R-class chassis were scrapped, their 1935 Weymann 30-seat bodies were salvaged and mounted on the chassis of thirty-one withdrawn coaches which were fitted with 7.7 litre oil engines at the same time. They were reclassified 11T11. The programme began with the prototype, T 396, in February 1938, which entered service at Reigate in March 1938. T 232 was the next conversion in June 1938 but it did not enter service until October and the main programme ran from October until December 1938. These were allocated to seven Country Bus garages, the largest numbers being at Two Waters (12), Watford (7) and Leatherhead (6). Five (T 208, 213, 215, 216 and 223) were repainted red in May 1939 for service on route 211 at Hanwell garage.

There were minor differences in the windscreen and dash of the T11 bodies transferred from the Reliances, compared with the T4 bodies mounted directly onto Regal chassis in 1935 (see page 37). Their radiators also projected further forward to accommodate the 7.7 litre oil engine. T 232B, which is about to pull away from the riverside stand at Staines West Station, is carrying its third Weymann body (see page 35), following its transformation in June 1938. J.F. Higham

The 9T9s were the first London Regals to have oil engines and preselective gearboxes, their mechanical specification being the same as the standard STLs. Weymann, who built the bodies, established itself as the main external supplier to the Country Bus department during the 1930s and built up a reputation for high quality workmanship. These were the first vehicles to have their front bulkhead linked to the wing assembly in a continuous sweep but unlike later vehicles this also incorporated the housing for the nearside headlamp. Unusually, the bonnet was part of the body structure which resulted in this unusual conjunction with the radiator. The first home of T 428c was Reigate garage, where this photograph was taken. D.A. Ruddom collection

In 1936 the LPTB purchased fifty thirty-seat front-entrance Weymann bodied Regals for Green Line service (T 403–452; classified 9T9). Their mechanical specification was similar to contemporary STLs and they were London's first Regals with oil engines, preselective gearboxes and fluid flywheels. They had a new style of body which set the standard for the next three years and were notable for their integral bonnet and wing assembly, the continuous panelling running under the radiator shell, and their bumper bars. Internally they were completed to full Green Line standard with Clayton Dewandre heaters, luggage racks, deeper seat squabs, linoleum flooring and ash trays on the backs of seats. They first went into service in March 1936, operating on routes I, J, K1 and K2 from Crawley, Reigate, Watford (Leavesden Road), Dorking, Hatfield, Hitchin and Leatherhead and four running alongside the 6Q6s on the Q and R from Amersham. The 9T9s were demoted to bus work in 1939 but were nevertheless withdrawn and converted to public ambulances in September 1939.

As part of its large 1938/39 replacement programme London Transport ordered 266 AEC Regals (the 10T10 class) to replace all pre-1936 Green Line coaches. These employed the new AEC pot cavity 8.8 litre oil engine, which had been inspired by the similar engines supplied by Leyland in the STD class and were built under licence from the Lancashire company. They differed from the 9T9s in having a shorter wheelbase, an externally sliding platform door, a neater front end design and many other details but were generally similar in appearance and body specification. The bodywork was of composite construction, the first run of such bodies built in the shops at Chiswick. The first 150 had thirty seats but the last 116 were to a modified design with thirty-four seats. In these the bulkhead behind the entrance steps was removed and replaced by a panel extending up to waist level which extended slightly into the stairwell.

The first to be licensed was T 454 at Windsor and the last T 691 at Romford (London Road) in March 1939, by which time they were operating on twenty-one routes from twenty-three garages. All 266 were withdrawn on 1st September and converted to public ambulances in readiness for the declaration of war two days later. As tension eased, the Government approved some limited restoration of coach services and released 164 10T10s for service on 29th November. Twenty-one were allocated to Romford for the restoration of route Y2 on 13th December but the others were deployed as Country Buses until early 1940 to release buses borrowed from Central Buses.

The 10T10 coaches of 1938 marked an important step forward in the development of the mechanical specification by introducing the Board's new policy of having larger engines derated to improve efficiency and reduce wear and tear. The Chiswick-built bodywork repeated the overall pattern of the 9T9s but with important differences, particularly in the reversion to a conventional front end arrangement which was more compact and enabled the larger 8.8 litre engine to be fitted in without major changes to the body design. T 506c was a 'pure' 10T10 and entered service at Windsor, where it was photographed, in June 1938. J.F. Higham

T 598c leaves Eccleston Bridge soon after entering service at Staines garage in May 1938. Other differences from the 9T9 visible from this point of view, include the sliding door, which is in an open recess instead of sliding into the body, the straight sill of the front bulkhead window and the sharper curve at the front of the beading along the roof. Roy Marshall

Chassis:	AEC Regal 662 (T 1–215, 217–267, 269–273, 275–304, 306–324, 346–402); or O662 (T 216, 274, 305, 403–718); LGOC CB (T 1000–1002)
Engine:	AEC A140 6-cylinder 6.1 litre 95 bhp petrol (T 1–12, 14–50, 150–154, 156, 319–324, 358–369, 393–402); AEC A145 6-cylinder 7.4 litre 95 bhp petrol (T 13, 51–149, 155, 157–215, 217–267, 269–273, 275–304, 306–318, 346–357, 370–392)
	AEC A161 6-cylinder 8.8 litre indirect injection 130 bhp oil (T 216, 274, 305); AEC A173 6-cylinder 7.7 litre direct injection 95 bhp oil (11T11 class from 1938 – see fleet list); AEC A171 6-cylinder 7.7 litre 95 bhp oil (T 403–452); AEC A180 6-cylinder 8.8 litre direct injection 100 bhp oil (T 453–718); Meadows 6-cylinder 6.1 litre 85bhp petrol (T 1000–1002)[1]
Transmission:	AEC D124 four speed crash (T 1–306, 309–324, 346–402 range); Daimler D128 4-speed preselective with fluid flywheel (T 307–308)[2]; D132 direct selection preselective with fluid flywheel (T 403–718); three speed crash (T 1000–1002)
Bodywork:	LGOC (T 1–50, 156, 1000–1002); LGOC, Hall Lewis or Short Bros. (T 51–149, 155, 157–206); Duple, Ransomes Sims and Jefferies or Weymann (T 207–231, 233–306);
	Thos. Tilling (T 307–318); Dodson (T 391–392);
	Hall Lewis (T 319–324, 371–379, 383–390, 393–402); Hoyal (T 150–154); London Lorries (T 346–357)[3]; Strachan (T 358, 359, 361, 362, 364–366); Harrington (T 360, 363, 367, 368); Park Royal (T 369)[4];
	Short Bros. (T 370)[5]; Weymann (T 232, 380–382, 403–452; also 11T11 type (see fleet list); LPTB (T 453–718).
Capacity:	B28F (T 307–318); B29F (T 1000–1002); B30F (T 380–382); B30R[6] (T 1–37, 39–50, 156, 369[4], 371–378, 383–390;
	B32R (T 370)[5]; C27R (T 51–149, 155, 157–206); C28R (T 38); C29R (T 393–398); C30R (T 358); C31R (T 346–357, 360, 363); C32R (T 359, 361–362, 364–366); C29F (T 319–324);
	C30F (T 207–306); C32F (T 367–368); DP30F (T403–452); DP30 or 34F (T 453–718)
L.T. codes:	1T1 (T 4, 5, 9–12, 14, 17, 18, 20, 22–24, 29–32, 37, 41, 42, 44, 46–48, 50, 156; 1/1T1 (T 1, 2, 6, 7, 28, 33, 34, 39, 40; 2/1T1 (T 3, 8, 16, 19, 27, 36, 45, 49; 3/1T1 (T 13);
	5/1T1/1 (T 15, 21, 25, 26, 35); 4/1T6 (T 369–390)[5]; 2T2 (T 43); 3T3 (T 309–318); 4T3/1 (T 307–308)[2]; 5T4 T 346–351)[3]; 6T5 (T 352–357)[3]; 7T7 (T 38, 51–149, 155, 157–206); 1/7T7/1 (T 207–215, 217–231, 233–267, 269–273, 275–304, 306); 1/7T7/2 (T 232); 2/7T7/1 (T 216, 274, 305); 8T8 (T 150–154)
	8T8/1 (T 319–324, 399–402); 8T8/2 (T 393–398); 1/8T8/3 (T 358–368); 2/8T8/4 (T 391, 392); 9T9 (T 403–452);
	1/10 or 10T/T10 or 10/1 (T 453–718); 11T11 (see fleet list)
Built:	1929 (T 1–37, 41, 42, 44–46, 371); 1930 (T 38–40, 43, 47–215, 217–221, 223–225, 229, 230, 234, 235, 238, 245, 346–351, 358, 360, 363, 371–379, 383–390, 393–398); 1931 (T 216, 222, 226–228, 231–233, 236–237, 239–244, 246–306, 319–324, 352–357, 361, 362, 364, 380–382, 391, 392, 399–402, 1000–1002; 1932 (T 307–318, 359, 365–368, 369; 1933 (T 370); 1936 (T 403–452); 1938/39 (T 453–718)

Number built or acquired (by 31.12.39): 700
Number in stock: 1.7.33 370   31.12.39: 511

---

1 Meadows engines replaced by AEC A140 type between December 1932 and November 1933.
2 Converted to D124 in May and September 1934 respectively and reclassified 3T3.
3 Rebodied 1935 with new Weymann B26F bodies, all classified 5T4; capacity increased to B30F between February 1938 and April 1939.
4 Rebodied in September 1936 with T7/1 body, reclassified 1/7T7/1.
5 T 370 rebodied with Tilling B30F and reclassified 4/1T3 September 1936
6 T 1–14, 16–20, 22–24, 26–34, 36, 37, 39–50 and 156 converted to B30F by March 1935.

Where there is no date given for 'Date into stock', the vehicle was acquired on vesting day, 1st July 1933 from the LGOC or one of the other Underground Group companies, except that T 369 and 371 were from Watford & District which was acquired by LGCS on 1.7.33.

T		Date out of stock	T		Date out of stock	T		Date out of stock
1	UU6616		70	GF7281	16.12.38	139	GH623	12.9.38
2	UU6617		71	GF536	16.12.38	140	GF592	19.8.38
3	UU6618		72	GF505	9.9.38	141	GF563	17.8.38
4	UU6619		73	GF7277	17.3.39	142	GF523	7.3.39
5	UU6620		74	GF533	16.8.38	143	GF564	20.7.38
6	UU6621		75	GF561	17.3.39	144	GF519	13.12.38
7	UU6622		76	GF521		145	GF517	
8	UU6623		77	GF7282	16.12.38	146	GH626	12.9.38
9	UU6624		78	GF539	17.3.39	147	GF567	7.12.38
10	UU6625		79	GF549	20.9.38	148	GF593	15.9.38
11	UU6626		80	GF559	5.5.38	149	GF572	15.9.38
12	UU6627		81	GF508	30.1.39	150	GF483	10.3.38
13	UU6628		82	GF506	12.9.38	151	GF482	18.3.38
14	UU6629		83	GF584	3.10.38	152	GF481	11.3.38
15	UU6630		84	GF537	26.1.39	153	GF480	18.3.38
16	UU6631		85	GF7278		154	GF479	18.3.38
17	UU6632		86	GF597	21.7.38	155	GF525	6.5.38
18	UU6633		87	GF579	7.12.38	156	GF7251	
19	UU6634		88	GF7283	1.3.39	157	GF575	27.2.39
20	UU6635		89	GF543	18.3.39	158	GF589	12.5.38
21	UU6636		90	GF7279	24.8.38	159	GF588	
22	UU6637		91	GF510	18.8.38	160	GF573	
23	UU6638		92	GH625	28.2.39	161	GH3881	10.1.39
24	UU6639		93	GF515	22.2.39	162	GF576	17.3.39
25	UU6640	24.2.39	94	GF580		163	GH614	
26	UU6641		95	GF555	2.1.39	164	GF591	
27	UU6642		96	GF544	7.9.38	165	GF574	
28	UU6643		97	GF560	7.9.38	166	GF590	7.3.39
29	UU6644		98	GF7284	30.8.38	167	GH3887	
30	UU6645		99	GF583	27.2.39	168	GH3885	27.2.39
31	UU6646		100	GF511	9.9.38	169	GH3886	
32	UU6647		101	GF582		170	GH3884	16.1.39
33	UU6648		102	GF7276	26.1.39	171	GH3882	
34	UU6649		103	GF512	2.1.39	172	GH3883	
35	UU6650	30.3.39	104	GF550	18.8.38	173	GH8002	1.3.39
36	UU6651		105	GF585	30.12.38	174	GH8003	
37	UU6652		106	GF598	16.1.39	175	GH8005	
38	UU6653		107	GF565	26.9.38	176	GH8001	
39	UU6654		108	GF586		177	GH615	24.2.39
40	UU6655		109	GF599		178	GH8004	
41	UU6656		110	GF503	7.9.38	179	GH611	12.1.39
42	UU6657		111	GF551		180	GH612	
43	UU6658		112	GF600	17.3.39	181	GH616	
44	UU6659		113	GF7280		182	GH3814	
45	UU6660		114	GF587		183	GH617	23.2.39
46	UU6661		115	GF571	7.3.39	184	GH618	
47	UU6662		116	GF509		185	GH613	17.3.39
48	UU6663		117	GF507	17.3.39	186	GH3810	7.9.38
49	UU6664		118	GF502		187	GH619	28.2.39
50	UU6665		119	GF547	21.7.38	188	GH3815	28.2.39
51	GF526		120	GF557		189	GH8090	6.3.39
52	GF504	13.12.38	121	GF594		190	GH3812	17.3.39
53	GF542	9.1.39	122	GF516	16.8.38	191	GH3811	30.12.38
54	GF531	14.2.39	123	GF570	18.3.39	192	GH622	7.12.38
55	GF541	5.9.38	124	GF568		193	GH3816	25.1.39
56	GF540		125	GH624	10.8.38	194	GH3817	3.5.38
57	GF529	7.12.38	126	GH621	18.8.38	195	GF577	2.1.39
58	GF530	21.2.39	127	GF595	18.5.38	196	GH3818	23.1.39
59	GF534	18.3.39	128	GF548	21.2.39	197	GH3813	3.5.38
60	GF527	20.7.38	129	GF558	7.12.38	198	GH8090	21.1.39
61	GF538		130	GF513	23.1.39	199	GH620	
62	GF528	7.12.38	131	GF546	7.12.38	200	GH8091	25.1.39
63	GF532	17.3.39	132	GF566		201	GH8092	21.1.39
64	GF581	21.7.38	133	GF562	5.12.38	202	GH8093	10.1.39
65	GF596	17.3.39	134	GF518	18.8.38	203	GH8094	
66	GF501		135	GF569	17.3.39	204	GH8095	14.2.39
67	GF522	18.3.39	136	GF545		205	GF578	21.1.39
68	GF524	5.9.38	137	GF520	26.9.38	206	GH3819	
69	GF535	10.1.39	138	GF514	27.2.39	207	GK5493	

T		Date out of stock	T		Date out of stock
* 208	GH8096		273	GN4683	
209	GK5490		274	GN2177	
210	GN2007	s 15.6.39	* 275	GK3177	
211	GK5487		* 276	GH3825	
* 212	GK5492		277	GK3180	
* 213	GN2016		278	GH3826	s 20.4.39
* 214	GK3181		279	GH8097	s .6.39
* 215	GK5488		* 280	GN4647	
* 216	GN2176		281	GK3171	
217	GN2002		282	GN4648	s 26.5.39
218	GK3183		* 283	GN2104	
219	GK5486		284	GK3178	s 6.5.39
220	GN2015	18.3.39	* 285	GH8098	
221	GN2003	s 18.7.39	286	GN2179	
222	GH3828	7.3.39	287	GN2191	c 18.10.39
* 223	GK5491		288	GN2103	
224	GK3184	18.10.39	289	GH3827	6.9.38
225	GK3182	28.2.39	290	GN2106	
* 226	GN2018		291	GN2105	
227	GN2006	s 3.7.39	292	GN2108	
228	GH3802	6.9.38	293	GK5499	
229	GK5494		294	GH8100	s 25.5.39
230	GK5495		295	GN4682	
231	GH3805		* 296	GN4684	
* 232	GH3803		297	GN2107	
233	GK3188		* 298	GN4672	
* 234	GK3185		299	GK3179	s 13.5.39
235	GK3186		300	GK3172	12.8.38
* 236	GN2080		301	GK3173	
* 237	GN2004		302	GN4671	
238	GN2008		303	GK3174	s 8.7.39
239	GN2005		304	GK3176	s 15.6.39
240	GN2020		305	GN2178	
241	GN2068	8.7.39	306	GN4673	
242	GH3829	s 3.7.39	307	GY8419	
243	GN2019	s 25.5.39	308	GY8408	
244	GH3888		309	GY8409	
245	GN2001	s 18.7.39	310	GY8410	
246	GK3189	s 15.6.39	311	GY8411	
247	GN2021	28.2.39	312	GY8412	
248	GN2017		313	GY8413	
249	GK3190		314	GY8414	
* 250	GN2069		315	GY8415	
251	GH3889		316	GY8416	
252	GH3801		317	GY8417	
* 253	GH3807		318	GY8418	
254	GH3806	28.2.39	319	PL6471	sb (15.2.38)
* 255	GK5497		320	PL6472	sb (21.2.38)
256	GK5496	s 18.7.39	321	PL6473	16.8.38
257	GH3800	s 26.5.39	322	PL6474	9.3.38
258	GN2024	s 2.9.39	323	PL6475	18.8.38
259	GH3804	s 10.6.39	324	PL6476	17.5.38
260	GN2079	s 15.6.39	325–345		numbers not used
* 261	GN2023		346	GF5135	
262	GH3890		347	GF5136	
263	GK3175		348	GJ8068	
264	GH3820		349	GJ8069	
265	GH3823		350	GJ8072	
* 266	GK3187		351	GJ8073	
* 267	GH3824		352	GN4416	
268	GK5498		353	GN8238	
269	GK3191	s 3.7.39	354	GN8239	
270	GH3821		355	GN8240	
* 271	GH3822		356	GN8241	
272	GH8099		357	GN8242	

T		Date into stock	Date out of stock	T		Date into stock
358	UR6564		12.7.38	423	CLX571	4.7.36
* 359	KX7886	1.10.33		424	CLX572	22.7.36
360	UR6801	1.10.33	3.5.38	425	CLX573	18.6.36
* 361	KX7634	1.10.33		426	CLX574	3.10.36
* 362	KX7635	1.10.33		427	CLX575	23.6.36
363	UR6802	1.10.33	12.7.38	428	CXX151	20.6.36
* 364	KX6785	1.10.33		429	CXX152	14.7.36
365	KX8643	1.10.33	30.3.39	430	CXX153	2.7.36
366	KX8644	1.10.33	21.2.39	431	CXX154	11.7.36
367	JH1915	1.10.33	21.2.39	432	CXX155	26.6.36
368	JH1916	1.10.33	3.5.38	433	CXX156	16.10.36
369	JH2101			434	CXX157	29.8.36
370	JH5101	10.11.33	c 13.10.39	435	CXX158	11.9.36
371	MY2276		c 13.10.39	436	CXX159	7.7.36
372	PG6780		c 17.10.39	437	CXX160	9.7.36
373	PG6781		c 17.10.39	438	CXX161	24.7.36
374	PG6782		24.2.39	439	CXX162	20.10.36
375	PG7507			440	CXX163	5.9.36
376	PG7508			441	CXX164	31.7.36
377	PG7509			442	CXX165	30.7.36
378	PG7510		17.3.39	443	CXX166	19.8.36
379	PG7511		c 13.10.39	444	CXX167	9.9.36
380	PL6456		7.3.39	445	CXX168	14.8.36
381	PL6457		15.9.38	446	CXX169	13.8.36
382	PL6458			447	CXX170	21.8.36
383	PG6783			448	CXX171	24.9.36
384	PG6784			449	CXX172	25.8.36
385	PG6785			450	CXX173	1.9.36
386	PG7025		1.3.39	451	CXX174	30.9.36
387	PG7503		8.12.38	452	CXX175	29.8.36
388	PG7504		c 13.10.39	453	ELP177	15.3.38
389	PG7505		22.2.39	454	ELP178	23.2.38
390	PG7506		13.7.38	455	ELP179	11.3.38
391	JH32			456	ELP180	24.3.38
392	JH33			457	ELP181	6.4.38
393	PG7681		sb (15.2.38)	458	ELP182	8.4.38
394	PG7682		21.7.38	459	ELP183	24.3.38
395	PG7683		12.5.38	460	ELP184	25.3.38
* 396	PG7839			461	ELP185	24.3.38
397	PG7840		17.3.38	462	ELP186	1.4.38
398	PG7841		12.7.38	463	ELP187	11.4.38
399	PL6467		13.7.38	464	ELP188	30.3.38
400	PL6468		17.8.38	465	ELP189	30.5.38
401	PL6469		17.3.38	466	ELP190	14.3.38
402	PL6470		11.3.38	467	ELP191	17.3.38
403	CLX551	9.6.36		468	ELP192	25.3.38
404	CLX552	4.6.36		469	ELP193	4.4.38
405	CLX553	26.5.36		470	ELP194	18.3.38
406	CLX554	25.6.36		471	ELP195	30.3.38
407	CLX555	29.5.36		472	ELP196	28.3.38
408	CLX556	4.6.36		473	ELP197	5.4.38
409	CLX557	5.6.36		474	ELP198	12.4.38
410	CLX558	11.6.36		475	ELP199	24.3.38
411	CLX559	16.9.36		476	ELP200	25.3.38
412	CLX560	28.7.36		477	ELP201	19.4.38
413	CLX561	22.10.36		478	ELP202	17.3.38
414	CLX562	13.6.36		479	ELP203	7.4.38
415	CLX563	18.9.36		480	ELP204	4.4.38
416	CLX564	19.9.36		481	ELP205	6.4.38
417	CLX565	14.9.36		482	ELP206	7.4.38
418	CLX566	21.5.36		483	ELP207	3.4.38
419	CLX567	16.7.36		484	ELP208	19.4.38
420	CLX568	15.6.36		485	ELP209	6.4.38
421	CLX569	20.7.36		486	ELP210	24.3.38
422	CLX570	6.10.36		487	ELP211	24.3.38

T		Date into stock		T		Date into stock
488	ELP212	25.3.38		553	ELP277	13.6.38
489	ELP213	11.4.38		554	ELP278	26.5.38
490	ELP214	11.6.38		555	ELP279	26.5.38
491	ELP215	28.6.38		556	ELP280	28.5.38
492	ELP216	1.4.38		557	ELP281	27.5.38
493	ELP217	20.4.38		558	ELP282	31.5.38
494	ELP218	21.4.38		559	ELP283	27.5.38
495	ELP219	18.3.38		560	ELP284	8.6.38
496	ELP220	8.4.38		561	ELP285	1.6.38
497	ELP221	5.4.38		562	ELP286	1.6.38
498	ELP222	11.4.38		563	ELP287	30.5.38
499	ELP223	20.5.38		564	ELP288	3.6.38
500	ELP224	23.4.38		565	ELP289	23.7.38
501	ELP225	29.4.38		566	EYK201	3.6.38
502	ELP226	26.4.38		567	EYK202	2.6.38
503	ELP227	18.5.38		568	EYK203	7.6.38
504	ELP228	5.4.38		569	EYK204	4.6.38
505	ELP229	13.4.38		570	EYK205	10.6.38
506	ELP230	11.5.38		571	EYK206	9.6.38
507	ELP231	25.4.38		572	EYK207	20.6.38
508	ELP232	25.4.38		573	EYK208	10.6.38
509	ELP233	26.4.38		574	EYK209	14.6.38
510	ELP234	22.4.38		575	EYK210	20.6.38
511	ELP235	7.5.38		576	EYK211	21.6.38
512	ELP236	27.4.38		577	EYK212	17.6.38
513	ELP237	12.5.38		578	EYK213	29.6.38
514	ELP238	20.4.38		579	EYK214	21.6.38
515	ELP239	22.4.38		580	EYK215	30.6.38
516	ELP240	11.5.38		581	EYK216	23.6.38
517	ELP241	29.4.38		582	EYK217	16.6.38
518	ELP242	21.4.38		583	EYK218	18.6.38
519	ELP243	28.4.38		584	EYK219	27.6.38
520	ELP244	27.4.38		585	EYK220	24.6.38
521	ELP245	18.5.38		586	EYK221	6.7.38
522	ELP246	23.8.38		587	EYK222	7.7.38
523	ELP247	2.5.38		588	EYK223	24.6.38
524	ELP248	12.5.38		589	EYK224	29.6.38
525	ELP249	26.4.38		590	EYK225	27.6.38
526	ELP250	1.7.38		591	EYK226	7.7.38
527	ELP251	28.4.38		592	EYK227	4.7.38
528	ELP252	3.5.38		593	EYK228	1.7.38
529	ELP253	17.5.38		594	EYK229	29.6.38
530	ELP254	14.5.38		595	EYK230	30.6.38
531	ELP255	10.5.38		596	EYK231	6.7.38
532	ELP256	30.4.38		597	EYK232	2.7.38
533	ELP257	23.5.38		598	EYK233	1.7.38
534	ELP258	19.5.38		599	EYK234	14.7.38
535	ELP259	9.5.38		600	EYK235	4.7.38
536	ELP260	24.5.38		601	EYK236	8.7.38
537	ELP261	25.5.38		602	EYK237	12.7.38
538	ELP262	9.5.38		603	EYK238	15.6.38
539	ELP263	10.5.38		604	EYK239	17.6.38
540	ELP264	2.5.38		605	EYK240	22.6.38
541	ELP265	19.5.38		606	EYK241	21.6.38
542	ELP266	20.5.38		607	EYK242	21.7.38
543	ELP267	9.5.38		608	EYK243	11.7.38
544	ELP268	25.5.38		609	EYK244	8.7.38
545	ELP269	5.5.38		610	EYK245	9.7.38
546	ELP270	10.5.38		611	EYK246	12.7.38
547	ELP271	16.5.38		612	EYK247	28.7.38
548	ELP272	5.5.38		613	EYK248	20.7.38
549	ELP273	13.5.38		614	EYK249	13.7.38
550	ELP274	23.5.38		615	EYK250	13.7.38
551	ELP275	16.5.38		616	EYK251	19.8.38
552	ELP276	21.5.38		617	EYK252	18.7.38

T		Date into stock	T		Date into stock
618	EYK253	18.7.38	670	EYK305	22.9.38
619	EYK254	22.7.38	671	EYK306	19.9.38
620	EYK255	26.7.38	672	EYK307	27.9.38
621	EYK256	16.7.38	673	EYK308	29.9.38
622	EYK257	21.7.38	674	EYK309	14.9.38
623	EYK258	25.7.38	675	EYK310	5.10.38
624	EYK259	19.7.38	676	EYK311	3.10.38
625	EYK260	2.9.38	677	EYK312	17.9.38
626	EYK261	17.8.38	678	EYK313	20.9.38
627	EYK262	29.7.38	679	EYK314	14.10.38
628	EYK263	27.7.38	680	EYK315	1.10.38
629	EYK264	15.8.38	681	EYK316	5.10.38
630	EYK265	25.7.38	682	EYK317	10.10.38
631	EYK266	8.8.38	683	EYK318	12.10.38
632	EYK267	26.7.38	684	EYK319	13.10.38
633	EYK268	18.8.38	685	EYK320	15.10.38
634	EYK269	19.8.38	686	EYK321	20.10.38
635	EYK270	15.8.38	687	EYK322	19.10.38
636	EYK271	8.8.38	688	EYK323	21.10.38
637	EYK272	15.8.38	689	EYK324	17.10.38
638	EYK273	9.8.38	690	EYK325	22.10.38
639	EYK274	26.8.38	691	EYK326	25.3.39
640	EYK275	1.9.38	692	EYK327	29.10.38
641	EYK276	17.8.38	693	EYK328	31.10.38
642	EYK277	22.8.38	694	EYK329	25.10.38
643	EYK278	2.9.38	695	EYK330	1.11.38
644	EYK279	22.8.38	696	EYK331	24.10.38
645	EYK280	29.8.38	697	EYK332	4.11.38
646	EYK281	23.8.38	698	EYK333	27.10.38
647	EYK282	3.9.38	699	EYK334	2.11.38
648	EYK283	31.8.38	700	EYK335	16.11.38
649	EYK284	24.8.38	701	EYK336	2.11.38
650	EYK285	18.8.38	702	EYK337	10.11.38
651	EYK286	6.9.38	703	EYK338	28.10.38
652	EYK287	25.8.38	704	EYK339	11.11.38
653	EYK288	30.8.38	705	EYK340	5.11.38
654	EYK289	24.8.38	706	EYK341	3.11.38
655	EYK290	27.8.38	707	EYK342	5.12.38
656	EYK291	8.9.38	708	EYK343	9.11.38
657	EYK292	12.9.38	709	EYK344	12.11.38
658	EYK293	9.9.38	710	EYK345	23.11.38
659	EYK294	5.9.38	711	EYK346	5.12.38
660	EYK295	13.9.38	712	EYK347	17.11.38
661	EYK296	10.9.38	713	EYK348	14.11.38
662	EYK297	7.9.38	714	EYK349	7.11.38
663	EYK298	30.9.38	715	EYK350	28.11.38
664	EYK299	21.9.38	716	EYK351	19.11.38
665	EYK300	26.9.38	717	EYK352	31.12.38
666	EYK301	16.9.38	718	EYK353	21.11.38
667	EYK302	23.9.38	1000	GO7153	†
668	EYK303	24.9.38	1001	GT7446	†
669	EYK304	15.9.38	1002	GT7447	†

c Date chassis scrapped; body scrapped earlier
s Converted to service vehicle
sb Date body scrapped; chassis mounted as lorries: T 319 6.38 (112W), T 320 3.38 (114W), T393 4.38 (113W)
* Converted to 11T11 type in 1938
† Still in stock or licensed on 31.12.39. Sold 26.8.40 (T 1000), 28.8.40 (T 1001/2)

TD

Although the Leyland Titan was designed for double-deckers, 21 single-deck buses and coaches mounted on that chassis were acquired by London Transport. Nineteen, all but one of which were coaches, came from Premier Line who ran Green Line-type services between London, Slough, Farnham Common and Windsor. Premier also contributed 20 Tigers (TR class). The two other buses (TD 86 and 131) came from two London Independents, R. Hawkins & Co. and the Prince Omnibus Co, and therefore went into the Central Bus fleet at first. They did not enter service there but were transferred almost immediately to Country Buses at Northfleet and Windsor garages respectively. The remainder, which had gone into the Country Bus & Coach fleet, were numbered in the Green Line L series until renumbered as TDs in 1935. The TDs were all fitted with standard-size route and destination indicator boxes but were otherwise not modified in any significant way.

The TD coaches were allocated at first to Slough (Bath Road), with some being transferred for a time to Staines. When the new Windsor garage opened in December 1937 the TDs went there and continued in service until the arrival of the 10T10 coaches in 1938. While the early deliveries of the Ts were taking place, some TD coaches were dispersed to Addlestone, Dunton Green and Staines garages and, for a short time, to Leatherhead. They were withdrawn from service between December 1937 and May 1938 (including the buses) and sold later that year. Many found willing buyers among bus and coach operators and a few became lorries or showmen's vehicles.

TD 131B had been a bus with the Prince Omnibus Company and had come to the Country department via Central Buses, so always carried that number. Although the body shell was the same, the Duple bus body differed from its coach design in a number of ways, examples being the use of half-drop windows and plain metal rainshields instead of shaped glass. There was also no emergency door as the bus had an open platform.
J.F. Higham Collection

All but one of the single-deck TDs had Duple bodywork, which was the favourite of Premier Line Ltd. Dressed in London Transport's first coach livery, this 1930 vintage Titan carries the Green Line fleet number L 30, which was changed to TD 189 when Chiswick took control of such matters in 1935.
J.F. Higham

TD 86B, was the odd-one-out in having a Birch 30-seat bus body dating from 1930. It is at Slough GWR station standing alongside one of the former Lewis Short Bros-bodied STs. J.F. Higham

Chassis: Leyland Titan TD1
Engine: Leyland 6-cylinder 6.8 litre ohc 98 bhp petrol
Transmission: Leyland 4-speed crash
Bodywork: Birch (TD 86); Duple (TD 131, 132, 174–191)
Capacity: C28R (TD 177, 182, 183, 188, 190); C26R (TD 132, 174, 175, 178–181, 184–187, 189); C25R (TD 176); B31R (TD 131); B30R (TD 86); B28R (TD 191)
L.T. codes: Not allocated
Built: 1929 (TD 174–180, 191); 1930 (TD 86, 132, 181–190); 1931 (TD 131)
Number acquired: 21
Number in stock 1.7.33: Nil   31.12.39: Nil   Last out of stock: 1.9.38

		Green Line No.	Acquired from	Date into stock	Date out of stock
86	GH7079		R.Hawkins & Co. Ltd (Nil Desperandum, Peckham)	12.6.34	1.9.38
131	MV1019		Prince Omnibus Co. Ltd, Edmonton	4.12.34	1.9.38
132	GC1213	L 47	The Premier Line Ltd, Slough	20.12.33	13.7.38
174	GC1205	L 15	The Premier Line Ltd, Slough	20.12.33	11.7.38
175	GC1207	L 16	The Premier Line Ltd, Slough	20.12.33	11.7.38
176	GC1208	L 17	The Premier Line Ltd, Slough	20.12.33	16.5.38
177	GC1209	L 18	The Premier Line Ltd, Slough	20.12.33	11.7.38
178	GC1210	L 19	The Premier Line Ltd, Slough	20.12.33	13.7.38
179	GC1211	L 20	The Premier Line Ltd, Slough	20.12.33	13.7.38
180	GC1212	L 21	The Premier Line Ltd, Slough	20.12.33	6.5.38
181	GC6846	L 22	The Premier Line Ltd, Slough	20.12.33	9.5.38
182	GC6847	L 23	The Premier Line Ltd, Slough	20.12.33	3.5.38
183	GC7775	L 24	The Premier Line Ltd, Slough	20.12.33	15.7.38
184	GC7776	L 25	The Premier Line Ltd, Slough	20.12.33	3.5.38
185	GC7778	L 26	The Premier Line Ltd, Slough	20.12.33	15.7.38
186	GJ372	L 27	The Premier Line Ltd, Slough	20.12.33	14.7.38
187	GJ373	L 28	The Premier Line Ltd, Slough	20.12.33	13.7.38
188	GJ2350	L 29	The Premier Line Ltd, Slough	20.12.33	15.7.38
189	GJ2397	L 30	The Premier Line Ltd, Slough	20.12.33	9.5.38
190	GJ2398	L 31	The Premier Line Ltd, Slough	20.12.33	3.5.38
191	GC1206		The Premier Line Ltd, Slough	20.12.33	13.7.38

TR 1ʙ, on alien ground at Slough station, was one of only two Tiger TS4s acquired by London Transport. It had a Dodson 30-seat body dating from 1932. D.W.K. Jones

TR

The Leyland Tiger was the single-deck counterpart of the Titan and was introduced in 1927. The TS1 and the two models which followed soon afterwards, the TS2 and TS3 were all mechanically identical, the differences being in the length of bodywork for which they were designed and their wheelbases. The TS1 was intended for an overall body length of 27ft 6in, the TS2 and the TS3 for 26ft 0in. The TS1 and TS2 both had a 17ft 6in wheelbase while the TS3 was 16ft 6in. These variations in dimension were necessary to cater for the differing requirements of local authorities and the Police before the regulations were brought onto a standard national basis under the 1930 Road Traffic Act. All three models were powered by the same 98 bhp 6-cylinder 6.8 litre overhead camshaft petrol engine as the TD1 and transmission was through a four-speed sliding mesh gearbox. The TS4 was introduced in 1931 in the wake of the 1930 Act and was designed, like the Titan TD2, with the new standard national regulations in mind. A standard wheelbase of 17ft 6in was now possible, the permitted overall length of the body now being 27ft 6in. The TS4 included the improvements made to the contemporary Titan TD2, notably the larger 7.6 litre engine.

London Transport acquired a total of 42 Tigers, 31 of them coaches, all four models being represented. Eleven came into its hands on vesting day, eight from Maidstone & District and three which had been acquired by London General Country Services when they bought the businesses of C. Aston and The Chiltern Omnibus Service in May 1933. These and all the coaches subsequently taken over before 1935, were numbered in the Green Line L series but were renumbered into the TR class in 1935, along with those that had remained unnumbered until then. The largest single intake of Tigers was in December 1933, 20 from Premier Line who operated the coaches alongside its Titans on the London coach services. Two buses included in this acquisition did not survive to be given TR numbers as they were sold to the Thames Valley Traction Co. in May 1934 for operation on the Slough to Maidenhead route. TR 1 was not taken into stock until November 1934 when the Reliance business was acquired, but received the first number in the series as it was a Central Bus until January 1935

The TS3 was marginally the most numerous in the LPTB fleet, most of them having come from Premier Line. TR 29c, a London Lorries-bodied example, is at Eccleston Bridge Victoria, the principal London gathering point for Green Line coaches. D.W.K. Jones

when it was transferred to Country Buses. By contrast, the four coaches taken over from the Prince Omnibus Co. on the same day were transferred immediately to Country Buses and received their numbers later (TR 32c–35c). The last five Tigers (TR36c–40c) came into the fleet in July 1935. These had been owned by Redcar Services of Tunbridge Wells who ran them on the coach service between their home town and London. Following a long period of negotiation about compensation terms between the LPTB and Redcar, the company was finally bought in February 1935 by Maidstone & District, who subsequently handed the coaches and the service over to London Transport.

The TRs continued in service until the arrival of the 10T10s in 1938, when they were withdrawn. Five continued in use for the 1938 summer season as Private Hire coaches based at Old Kent Road (TR 9,12, 14, 17 and 33). As the new TF coaches were expected for the 1939 season, these five were sold in November 1938. There were many ready buyers for these excellent coaches which saw further service for many years with companies outside London.

TR 33c, a Duple-bodied TS1, had been part of the Prince Omnibus Company's coastal express and excursion fleet and was taken into the Green Line fold when it was acquired by the LPTB. The prominent beading separating the side panels was one of the most distinctive features of these bodies. D.W.K. Jones

Not a French château but Slough GWR station is the setting for TR 7B after it had been sent to Langley Road garage to join other Leylands in the Country Bus fleet. It was the only Birch-bodied Tiger, a 30-seater bus new to St Albans & District in 1931. D.W.K. Jones

There were only two Thurgood-bodied Tigers both of which had been owned originally by C. Aston of Watford and had come to the LPTB via London General Country Services. The shallow indicator box of TR 9c was very distinctive and required a specially adapted blind which was evidently vulnerable to poor adjustment. J.F. Higham

When Maidstone & District bought this batch of Tigers in 1930 they referred to them as Pullman Saloon Coaches but TR 6ʙ became a bus in the Country fleet within a short time of being acquired. Slough was a honeypot for these Leylands because it had been the base of Premier Line who supplied twenty of the 42 acquired by the Board. D.W.K. Jones

Five of these Beadle-bodied TS2s came from Redcar Services in 1935, indirectly via Maidstone & District who had acquired the company. As yet unnumbered and still in Redcar colours at Eccleston Bridge, Victoria, TR 38c is still carrying its original boards and blinds but has been given its new fleet name. The narrow destination blind among the clutter of the front dash was unusual. J.F. Higham

Chassis: Leyland Tiger TS1 (TR 9, 10, 32, 33); TS2: (TR 6, 11–17, 34–40); TS3: (TR 2–5, 7, 19–31, GN5139, 5150); TS4 (TR 1, 8)

Engine: Leyland 6-cylinder 6.8 litre ohc 98 bhp petrol (TS1 TS2 and TS3); 7.6 litre ohc 98 bhp petrol (TS4)

Transmission: Leyland 4-speed crash

Bodywork: Beadle (TR 36–40); Dodson (TR 1); Short Bros. C31C (TR 6, 11–17); Thurgood (TR 9, 10); Birch B30R (TR 7); Duple (TR 2, 3, 18–21, 32–35) London Lorries (TR 4, 5, 8, 22–31, GN5139, 5150)

Capacity: B32R: (TR 2); B31R : (TR 1[1]); B30R (TR 7[2]); B26R (TR 4, 5); C32? (TR 8–10); C31C (TR 6[1], 11–17); C30? (TR 32, 33); C28D (TR 34, 35); C26R (TR 3, 18–31, GN5139, 5150); C26D (TR 36–40)

L.T. codes: Not allocated

Built: 1930: (TR 2–6, 11–27, 31, 34–40); 1931: (TR 7, 9, 10, 28–30, 32, 33, GN 5139, 5150); 1932: (TR 1, 8)

Number acquired: 42:

Number in stock 1.7.33: 11   31.12.39: Nil   Last out of stock: 7.11.38

[1] TR 1 and 6 were reseated to 30 in February 1936
[2] TR 7 was reseated to 31 in January 1936

		Green Line No.	Acquired from	Date into stock	Date out of stock
1	EV8334		Reliance Omnibus Co. Ltd, Chingford	6.11.34	2.9.38
2	GH7025		The Premier Line Ltd, Slough	20.12.33	14.7.38
3	GH7026	L 33	The Premier Line Ltd, Slough	20.12.33	5.5.38
4	GK5716		The Premier Line Ltd, Slough	20.12.33	13.7.38
5	GK5721		The Premier Line Ltd, Slough	20.12.33	6.5.38
6	KR6304	L 7	Maidstone & District Motor Services Ltd	1.7.33	2.9.38
7	UR9367		Charles Russett & Son (St Albans & District)	10.11.33	2.9.38
8	JH1921	L 4	LGCS Ltd (formerly Prentice & Son (Chiltern O'bus Service)	1.7.33	9.7.38
9	UR9621	L 5	LGCS Ltd (formerly C.Aston, Watford)	1.7.33	7.11.38
10	UR9622	L 6	LGCS Ltd (formerly C.Aston, Watford)	1.7.33	6.5.38
11	KR6301	L 8	Maidstone & District Motor Services Ltd	1.7.33	3.5.38
12	KR6302	L 9	Maidstone & District Motor Services Ltd	1.7.33	7.11.38
13	KR6303	L 11	Maidstone & District Motor Services Ltd	1.7.33	6.5.38
14	KR6305	L 12	Maidstone & District Motor Services Ltd	1.7.33	7.11.38
15	KR6307	L 13	Maidstone & District Motor Services Ltd	1.7.33	9.7.38
16	KR7405	L 14	Maidstone & District Motor Services Ltd	1.7.33	6.5.38
17	KR7415	L 10	Maidstone & District Motor Services Ltd	1.7.33	7.11.38
18	GH7024	L 32	The Premier Line Ltd, Slough	20.12.33	13.7.38
19	GH7027	L 34	The Premier Line Ltd, Slough	20.12.33	14.7.38
20	GH7028	L 35	The Premier Line Ltd, Slough	20.12.33	20.7.38
21	GH7029	L 36	The Premier Line Ltd, Slough	20.12.33	13.7.38
22	GH7085	L 37	The Premier Line Ltd, Slough	20.12.33	6.5.38
23	GK445	L 38	The Premier Line Ltd, Slough	20.12.33	6.5.38
24	GK446	L 39	The Premier Line Ltd, Slough	20.12.33	6.5.38
25	GK5714	L 40	The Premier Line Ltd, Slough	20.12.33	20.7.38
26	GK5715	L 41	The Premier Line Ltd, Slough	20.12.33	6.5.38
27	GK5719	L 42	The Premier Line Ltd, Slough	20.12.33	9.7.38
28	GN5138	L 43	The Premier Line Ltd, Slough	20.12.33	13.7.38
29	GN5140	L 44	The Premier Line Ltd, Slough	20.12.33	11.7.38
30	GN5148	L 45	The Premier Line Ltd, Slough	20.12.33	9.7.38
31	GK5720	L 46	The Premier Line Ltd, Slough	20.12.33	6.5.38
32	HX4137		Prince Omnibus Co. Ltd	6.11.34	1.9.38
33	HX4138		Prince Omnibus Co. Ltd	6.11.34	7.11.38
34	MY4664		Prince Omnibus Co. Ltd	6.11.34	9.7.38
35	MY5029		Prince Omnibus Co. Ltd	6.11.34	9.7.38
36	KR1170		Maidstone & District M.S.Ltd (formerly Redcar Services)	31.7.35	6.5.38
37	KR1166		Maidstone & District M.S.Ltd (formerly Redcar Services)	31.7.35	6.5.38
38	KR1167		Maidstone & District M.S.Ltd (formerly Redcar Services)	31.7.35	17.5.38
39	KR1168		Maidstone & District M.S.Ltd (formerly Redcar Services)	31.7.35	17.5.38
40	KR1169		Maidstone & District M.S.Ltd (formerly Redcar Services)	31.7.35	16.5.38
*	GN5139		The Premier Line Ltd, Slough	20.12.33	5.34
*	GN5150		The Premier Line Ltd, Slough	20.12.33	5.34

* Withdrawn and sold to Thames Valley for the Slough to Maidenhead route before numbers were allocated

The Dennis Arrow was the single-deck equivalent of the Lance for a short period and had the same long radiator and other chassis features. The four vehicles in this class had all come from Red Rover via Green Line Coaches Ltd, who bought the company in 1932, and there were two makes of body. DL 38, at Wembley on a Private Hire outing, had this Thurgood body with an impressively wide sliding door but with perversely narrow saloon windows. D.W.K. Jones

DL

Four coaches mounted on Dennis Arrow chassis were renumbered into the DL class in 1935, having been numbered in the Green Line D series prior to that. Although the double-deck DLs were Lances, the Arrow was the single-deck equivalent of that chassis and it was considered appropriate for them to be included in the same class. All four were acquired from Red Rover Saloon Coaches of Aylesbury by London General Country Services Ltd in November 1932 and were allocated for Green Line duties. They continued in this role and as buses until being withdrawn from service in 1937.

Chassis:	Dennis Arrow
Engine:	Dennis 6-cylinder 6.1 litre 100 bhp petrol
Transmission:	Dennis 4-speed crash
Bodywork:	Birch (DL 36, 37); Thurgood (DL 38, 39)
Capacity:	C28F (DL 37); C30F (DL 38, 39); C32R (DL 36)*
L.T. codes:	Not allocated
Built:	1930 (DL 36); 1931 (DL 37–39)
Number acquired:	4
Number in stock 1.7.33: 4	31.12.39: Nil Last in stock: 18.3.38

* DL 36, 37, 39 later had their seating altered to 29

		Green Line No.	Acquired from	Date into stock	Date out of stock
36	GK8715	D 3	LGCS (formerly E.M., W.C. & R.A. Cain (Red Rover Saloon Coaches), Aylesbury	1.7.33	10.3.38
37	GN4490	D 1	"	1.7.33	10.3.38
38	GT1564	D 4	"	1.7.33	18.3.38
39	GT1657	D 5	"	1.7.33	10.3.38

Note: Two Dennis Lancet coaches and two buses were at first given the numbers DL 29, 30, 34, 35 but were later renumbered DT 4–7 (see section on minor bus types).

DA

Dennis Bros. of Guildford introduced its new lightweight bus chassis called the Dart in 1929 to replace its G-type model. It was a more powerful machine, incorporating a new six-cylinder engine capable of developing 70 bhp and was ideal for the expanding network of one-man operated routes in the outer suburbs of London. The LGOC therefore adopted it as its standard small bus between 1930 and 1933, buying a total of forty-two, all bodied at Chiswick Works. DA 1–32 were 7ft 2ins wide with eighteen inward facing seats and were delivered in two batches of twenty and twelve. DA 33–40 had the same dimensions but had an improved body layout with three rows of transverse seats at the rear and the remaining six seats arranged longitudinally. DA 41 and 42 were 6ft 6ins wide seventeen seaters for operation on route 211 where clearances in West Ealing were particularly tight.

Three Metcalfe bodied twenty-seaters were added to the London Transport fleet, numbered DA 43–45, when the business of the Romford and District Omnibus Co. Ltd was acquired in July 1934.

The DAs continued as a substantial part of the Central Bus one-man fleet but in slowly diminishing numbers as routes became busier and were converted to larger two-man types. By June 1939 only thirty-two were required for service, many only to meet the requirements of the Saturday schedules, and these were replaced before the end of the year, either by larger buses or, directly or indirectly, by the new CR class. The last two were delicensed on 1st December 1939 and forty-one remained in stock awaiting disposal at the end of that year.

Chassis: Dennis Dart
Engine: Dennis 6-cylinder 70 bhp petrol
Transmission: Dennis 4-speed crash
Bodywork: DA 1–42 LGOC (Chiswick); DA 43–45 Metcalfe
Capacity: B17F (DA 41–42); B18F (DA 1–40); B20F (DA 43–45)
L.T. chassis codes: 1DA (DA 1–32); 2DA (DA 33–40); 3DA (DA 41, 42)[1]
L.T. body codes: DA1 (DA 1–20); DA2 (DA 21–32); DA3 (DA 33–40); DA4 (DA 41, 42)[1]
Built: 1930 (DA 1–21); 1931 (DA22–32, 43); 1932 (DA 33–38, 44); 1933 (DA 39–42, 45)
Number acquired: 45
Number in stock: 1.7.33: 42   31.12.39: 41
[1] Codes were not allocated to DA 43–45, which were acquired from Roberts & Hammer (Romford & District)

All acquired from LGOC on 1.7.33 except 43–45

DA		DA		Date out of stock	DA		Date into stock	Date out of stock
1	GF494	16	GK3090		31	GO618		
2	GF493	17	GK3100		32	GO661		
3	GF492	18	GK3101		33	GX5325		
4	GF491	19	GK3108		34	GX5326		
5	GF7207	20	GK3132		35	GX5331		
6	GF7216	21	GK5342		36	GX5327		
7	GH8078	22	GK5441		37	GX5332		
8	GH8079	23	GK5442	2.3.39	38	GX5333		
9	GH8080	24	GN2145	16.3.39	39	JJ4333		
10	GH8081	25	GN2146		40	JJ4334		
11	GH8082	26	GN4738		41	JJ4373		
12	GK3049	27	GN4739		42	JJ4374		
13	GK3050	28	GN4740		43	EV4011	10.7.34	
14	GK3070	29	GN4741	16.3.39	44	EV5909	10.7.34	
15	GK3075	30	GN4742		45	ANO794	10.7.34	14.5.38

The 1DA1s had eighteen seats arranged longitudinally around the saloon, as can be glimpsed through the windows of DA 14, and the earlier examples of the type also had a lower bonnet and deeper windscreen than the remainder. Darts were normally Central Buses but there were regular weekend loans to Hertford which may be why DA 14 is in Hertford Bus Station on route 333. However, in July 1938 emergency changes to route 333 caused by a weak bridge increased the need for small buses at Hertford, which might have been the occasion of this photograph. Prior to that date the 333 was worked by the T class. J.F. Higham

The 2DA3s had a higher driving position and an improved internal layout with the rear three rows of seats in forward-facing pairs. Externally they had the modified front end with a shallower windscreen and squared-off dash. Although the Richings Park section of route 220 was one of the last to be operated by Darts, this photograph of DA 35 in Uxbridge was taken before the Pinner service was taken over by Ts in January 1938.
Capital Transport collection

The two 3DA4s had special narrow bodywork to cope with the tight clearances on route 211 through Gordon Road, Ealing and seated only seventeen. The different width is apparent in the lack of any overhang over the rear wheels on DA 41 at Haven Green, Ealing. These two buses also had the shallower windscreen and extended dash. J.F. Higham

The three Metcalfe-bodied Darts taken over from Romford & District had twenty seats arranged conventionally in forward facing pairs with inward facing seats over the rear wheel arches. The Darts continued to operate on former Romford & District route 252B, as two-man buses, until the route disappeared in the re-organisation of December 1936. DA 45 was the newest of the three, built in 1933. Capital Transport collection

The most numerous Central Bus single-deckers were the LTs, which were the three-axle equivalent of the 1T1 class with similarly styled Chiswick bodywork. LT 1120 is at Forest Hill on route 209, which became the 124 when double-decked in 1938. D.A. Ruddom collection

LT

A single-deck version of the LT was introduced by the LGOC in 1931, a total of 199 being built during that year. They replaced the remaining K-type single-deckers, the former London Public Dennises and the S type single-deckers, although some of these were returned to service later. Two more similar buses were built in 1932 for the newly formed London General Country Services Ltd. The chassis were the long wheelbase 664 version of the AEC Renown, which allowed the Chiswick bodies to be built to the maximum permitted length of thirty feet. Mechanically, they were similar to the double-deck version, except that they had the smaller 6.1 litre A140 AEC petrol engine, as used in the ST class, which developed 95 bhp.

Their bodies were a lengthened version of the T introduced a year earlier, the main differences being that the entrance was immediately behind the front wheels and the cab was rounded rather than square. The change in entrance position followed a shift of attitude by the Public Carriage Office which, until then, had insisted on rear entrances for two-man buses. The entrance was doorless, as required by the Metropolitan Police and this arrangement was to remain standard on all Central Bus single-deckers for the next twenty-two years. All but the last seventy-six for LGOC (classified LTL1/1 in 1934) and the two LGCS buses (LTL3) had no rear destination blind box. Instead a destination board was carried in a pair of slots at the bottom of the window of the rear emergency door. They had thirty-five seats, laid out as eleven forward facing doubles and two longitudinal seats over the rear wheel arches, seating six on the offside and five nearside. The two for LGCS, which became LT 1427 and 1428 in 1935, had lightweight seat frames of the same type as used in the Bluebird double-deckers. Although classified LTL under the 1934 scheme, all were numbered in the LT class.

One more Renown was acquired by London Transport, a thirty-seat Harrington bodied coach which came with the business of Edward Hillman's Saloon Coaches Ltd, in whose fleet it was unique. It was numbered LT 1429 and joined the Private Hire fleet until withdrawn in April 1939, after which it was placed in store at Bull Yard Peckham.

The buses were the most numerous class of single-decker in the Central Area and continued to cover about two-thirds of two-man single-deck requirements throughout this period. In the summer of 1939 they were to be found at fifteen of the twenty-three garages which ran single-deckers, the largest concentrations being at Muswell Hill (31 scheduled), Kingston (24) and Sutton (23).

The majority of single-deck LTs were 1LTL1s with no rear roller blind. Instead they had a destination board carried in slots on the rear emergency door and, in later years, a stencil route number above. LT 1186 has suffered a puncture at Golders Green in the early days of the war. Ken Glazier collection

The two Renowns which had been allotted to London General Country Services in 1932 remained in the Country Area throughout the period under review but their extra length limited their range of operation and for a time they were officially allocated only on Saturdays. LT 1427 in service at Dorking North station shows that the body design was identical to the LTL1/1, the only difference being that the seats were the lightweight type used on the contemporary Bluebirds. J. House

The only Renown acquired from an Independent by the LPTB was this handsome Harrington-bodied 32-seat coach, which was the sole AEC among a sea of Gilfords in the Edward Hillman fleet. It ran for the Private Hire department until 1939 when it became redundant with the arrival of the TFs. J.F. Higham

Chassis:	AEC Renown 664
Engine:	AEC A140 6-cylinder 6.1 litre 95bhp petrol
Transmission:	AEC D124 4 speed crash
Bodywork:	LGOC Chiswick (LT 1429 Harrington)
Capacity:	B35F; except LT 1429 (C32F)
L.T. chassis code:	1LTL (LT 1001–1201 range); 2LTL (LT 1427–1428); 3LTL (LT 1429).
L.T. Body codes:	LTL1 or 1/1 (LT 1001–1201 range); LTL3 (LT 1427–1428; LTL4 (LT 1429)
Built:	1931 (LT 1427–1429 1932)
Number acquired:	202
Number in stock:	1.7.33: 201; 31.12.39: 202

All acquired from LGOC or LGCS on 1.7.33 except LT 1429 (acquired from Edward Hillman's Saloon Coaches Ltd)

LT		LT		LT		
1001	GH8049	1070	GO5186	1139	GP3433	
1002	GN4775	1071	GO5174	1140	GP3422	
1003	GN4776	1072	GO7103	1141	GP3431	
1004	GO605	1073	GO5196	1142	GP3454	
1005	GO601	1074	GO5197	1143	GP3438	
1006	GN4784	1075	GO5199	1144	GP3434	
1007	GO606	1076	GO5198	1145	GP3437	
1008	GN4763	1077	GO7104	1146	GP3439	
1009	GN4783	1078	GO7141	1147	GP3436	
1010	GO637	1079	GO7102	1148	GP3448	
1011	GN4777	1080	GO7151	1149	GP3457	
1012	GO625	1081	GO7121	1150	GP3455	
1013	GO5114	1082	GO7116	1151	GP3485	
1014	GO614	1083	GO7119	1152	GT5005	
1015	GO648	1084	GO7129	1153	GT5002	
1016	GN4785	1085	GO7125	1154	GT5004	
1017	GO617	1086	GO7142	1155	GT5008	
1018	GO688	1087	GO7120	1156	GT5014	
1019	GO626	1088	GO7117	1157	GT5003	
1020	GO5113	1089	GO7118	1158	GT5006	
1021	GO607	1090	GO7128	1159	GT5015	
1022	GO641	1091	GO7135	1160	GT5007	
1023	GO631	1092	GO7148	1161	GT5013	
1024	GO630	1093	GO7149	1162	GT5016	
1025	GO650	1094	GO7145	1163	GT5022	
1026	GO689	1095	GO5200	1164	GT5030	
1027	GO649	1096	GO7152	1165	GT5029	
1028	GO629	1097	GO7155	1166	GT5028	
1029	GO644	1098	GO7144	1167	GT5027	
1030	GO628	1099	GO7146	1168	GT5033	
1031	GO638	1100	GO7147	1169	GT5031	
1032	GO640	1101	GO7150	1170	GT5032	
1033	GO627	1102	GO7161	1171	GT5034	
1034	GO655	1103	GO7165	1172	GT5046	
1035	GO642	1104	GO7159	1173	GT5052	
1036	GO639	1105	GO7163	1174	GT5047	
1037	GO672	1106	GO7167	1175	GT5044	
1038	GO643	1107	GO7171	1176	GT5045	
1039	GO668	1108	GO7166	1177	GT5054	
1040	GO656	1109	GO7158	1178	GT5053	
1041	GO684	1110	GO7162	1179	GT5059	
1042	GO671	1111	GO7160	1180	GT5060	
1043	GO666	1112	GO7172	1181	GT5061	
1044	GO669	1113	GO7173	1182	GT5079	
1045	GO651	1114	GO7186	1183	GT5062	
1046	GO667	1115	GO7181	1184	GT5074	
1047	GO673	1116	GO7179	1185	GT5072	
1048	GO670	1117	GO7184	1186	GT5080	
1049	GO665	1118	GO7180	1187	GT5075	
1050	GO685	1119	GO7177	1188	GT5076	
1052	GO5159	1120	GO7178	1189	GT5077	
1053	GO5169	1121	GO7185	1190	GT5078	
1054	GO5171	1122	GO7192	1191	GT5098	
1055	GO5161	1123	GP3402	1192	GT5090	
1056	GO5160	1124	GP3421	1193	GT5083	
1057	GO5162	1125	GP3401	1194	GT5145	
1058	GO5165	1126	GP3403	1195	GT5094	
1059	GO5170	1127	GP3406	1196	GT5107	
1060	GO5166	1128	GP3405	1197	GT5100	
1061	GO5167	1129	GP3404	1198	GT5101	
1062	GO5178	1130	GO7200	1199	GT5102	
1063	GO5173	1131	GP3407	1200	GT5108	
1064	GO5176	1132	GP3432	1201	GT5120	
1065	GO5187	1133	GP3425	1427	GX5337	
1066	GO5175	1134	GP3430	1428	GX5338	
1067	GO5185	1135	GP3435	1429	EV7340	13.8.34
1068	GO5192	1136	GP3420			
1069	GO5177	1138	GP3429			

BD

No Bedfords were bought by the LGOC or its subsidiaries but London Transport acquired a total of 25 from Independent operators in the Country Area under the terms of the 1933 Act and two with the business of Berkhamsted & District in 1939. Only 23 of these were numbered in the BD class, two having been withdrawn by Country Buses before its fleet was numbered and the two from Berkhamsted & District being delicensed and disposed of without entering service. The remainder were progressively withdrawn in line with the gradual decline in the number of small buses needed for service, the last eleven being delicensed in 1939. These remained in stock at the end of the year.

Chassis: Bedford WHB (JH2313); WHG (KX7894); WLB (BD 1–20, 22, 23, JH238, JH5324); WLG (BD 21)
Engine: Bedford 6-cylinder 3.18 litre 44 bhp petrol
Tranmsission: 4-speed crash
Bodywork: Duple (BD 3, 6, 7, 9, 10, 11, 12, 15, 20); Reall (BD 8); Strachan (BD 2, 13, 14); Thurgood (BD 17; JH238; JH2313; JH5324); Not known (1, 4, 5, 16, 18, 19, 21–23; KX7894)
Capacity: B14F (KX7894; JH2313); C20F (BD10); B20F remainder
L.T. chassis codes: Not allocated
L.T. body codes: Not allocated
Built: 1931 (BD 13, 14, 18, 19, 21, 22, KX7894; JH238);
                 1932 (BD 8, 11, 12, 15, 16, 17, 20, 23, JH2313);
                 1933 (BD 1–7, 9, 10, JH5324)
Number acquired: 27
Number in stock: 1.7.33: Nil   31.12.39: 11

		Acquired from	Date Into stock	Date out of stock
1	AGY485	H.M. Howells (Greenhithe & District Bus Services)	20.4.34	
2	AHK434	J.T.G. Smith & E. Godden (The Reliable Bus Service), South Stifford	30.5.34	.12.35 *
3	AKE725	H.M. Howells (Greenhithe & District Bus Services)	20.4.34	
4	AKK458	Gravesend & District Bus Services Ltd	14.10.33	.12.35 *
5	AKM308	H.D. Fletcher (The Enterprise Motor Service), Gravesend	13.11.33	8.7.38
6	AMF595	A.E. Warwick, Farnham Common	26.10.34	.12.35 *
7	AMH881	A.E. Warwick, Farnham Common	26.10.34	
8	AMY660	Mrs E.J. Coe (Purfleet Service Bus)	29.3.34	
9	APB940	J. Drake & H.P.Lucas (The Egham Motor Co)	16.2.34	
10	APC55	Sunshine Saloon Coaches Ltd, Kingston	29.12.33	
11	EV8977	J. Harvey (Harvey's Transport Bus Service), West Thurrock	9.3.34	.11.35 *
12	EV8978	J. Harvey (Harvey's Transport Bus Service), West Thurrock	9.3.34	2.3.39
13	JH550	F.J. Cobb (Albanian Bus Co), St Albans	16.2.34	8.7.38
14	JH911	F.J. Cobb (Albanian Bus Co) St Albans	16.2.34	4.3.39
15	JH974	A.R. Blowers (Express Motor Service), St Albans	2.1.34	
16	JH1300	E.A. Griffiths (Victoria Omnibus Service), St Albans	16.3.34	4.3.39
17	JH2314	A. Barnes (Reliance Coaches), St Albans	5.2.34	
18	KJ4255	H.D. Fletcher (The Enterprise Motor Service), Gravesend	14.11.33	8.7.38
19	KJ4256	H.D. Fletcher (The Enterprise Motor Service), Gravesend	14.11.33	8.7.38
20	MV6324	B. Dobson (Bluebell Services), Stanwell	9.3.34	
21	PJ1727	R.G. Harwood, Weybridge	16.1.34	
22	PJ1806	J. Drake & H.P.Lucas (The Egham Motor Co)	16.2.34	8.7.38
23	PJ8430	Sunshine Saloon Coaches Ltd, Kingston	29.12.33	
	KX7894	F. Berry, Slough	14.3.34	.12.34 †
	JH238	H.Aston (Berkhamsted & District Motor Services)	11.1.39	11.4.39
	JH2313	F.J. Cobb (Albanian Bus Co), St Albans	16.2.34	5.35
	JH5324	H.Aston (Berkhamsted & District Motor Services)	11.1.39	11.4.39

* Converted to vans for service vehicle fleet: 147B–150B (BD 2, 4, 6, 11 respectively).
† Body converted to truck by Country Buses.

Smith & Godden's Strachan-bodied Bedford has emigrated from the industrial landscape of south-west Essex to former Filkins and Ainsworth's more rural territory. It is working from Harefield garage on route 309A over former LUT tram track in Uxbridge High Street serving, among others, Woolworth's 3d and 6d store. Although built as recently as 1933, BD 2 did not last long as a bus, being converted to a van in December 1935. D.A. Ruddom collection

BD 13 also had Strachan bus body but of a more restrained no-nonsense style dating from 1931. It had been acquired from F.J. Cobb's Albanian Bus Co but had been sent further south to Windsor by London Transport. D.W.K. Jones

KX7894 was a 14-seat Bedford WHG which had been operated by F. Berry of Slough but spent only nine months in service with London Transport before being converted to a van. It was nevertheless painted in the new Country Bus livery with 'GENERAL' fleet name but no garage code or running number plates as these had not been introduced by Country Buses before it was withdrawn. J.F. Higham Collection

BD 8B was a Reall-bodied 20-seater which had been owned by Mrs Coe who ran it on the Grays – Purfleet road, where London Transport preferred double-deckers. It moved to St Albans and was still in stock at the end of 1939, though by then out of service. D.W.K. Jones

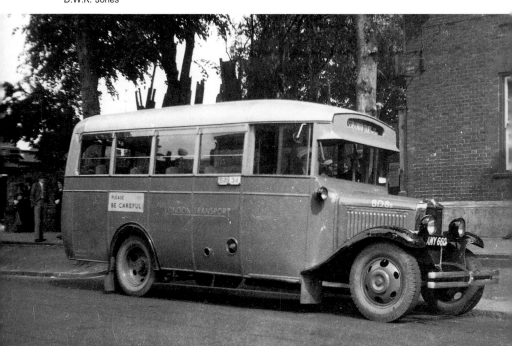

The builder of the utilitarian looking body of BD 5B has not been identified but the standard destination box with which it has been fitted and its garage and running number plates give it a typically London Transport look. It was acquired from Enterprise of Gravesend but the Board sent it across the river to Grays to operate on Rainham local route 375.
D.W.K. Jones

The classic Bedford/Duple combination is represented here by APB940 (later numbered BD 9B), a 20-seat WLB, new in 1933 and formerly owned by the Egham Motor Company. It was one of the last to be withdrawn and was still in stock at the end of 1939.
A.N. Porter

London Transport's first Leyland Cub was C 76B, a petrol-engined KP3, which came from St Albans and District and proved to be a milestone as its performance persuaded the LPTB to standardise on the model for its small bus needs. J.F. Higham

C

Leyland Motors Ltd introduced the Cub in 1931 as one of a range of light normal-control chassis which were built at its Kingston-upon-Thames factory. It was powered by a new six-cylinder 4.4 litre side valve petrol engine, had Lockheed hydraulic brakes and came in several wheelbases. London Transport acquired its first Cub with the business of Charles Russett and Son (St Albans and District) in November 1933 but, like all other Country Buses, it was not numbered until 1935 when it became C 76B. Satisfactory experience with this led the Board to inspect a Cub chassis (KP3 2257) between 15th and 22nd January 1934 and, on 1st February 1934 it authorised the purchase of one Leyland Cub KP3 for evaluation. This was its first single-deck purchase, because priority was being given to finding a replacement for the large variety of small single-deckers being acquired, mainly from operators in the Country Area.

C 1 was a KP3, with a wheelbase of 15ft 6ins, three feet greater than the Dennis Dart and capable of carrying a 7ft 6ins-wide body, four inches wider. This enabled the Chiswick-built composite body to have all twenty seats facing forward. The choice of the Cub was not a foregone conclusion, however. Before C 1 went into service the Board had formulated its first vehicle replacement plan, which envisaged a mixture of Thornycroft, Dennis Dart and Leyland Cub chassis but with a final decision on the Cubs deferred pending operational experience of C 1. By the time the Board came to make its final decision in 1935, Leyland had developed a new overhead valve pot cavity 4.4 litre oil engine for the model and this no doubt influenced London Transport's decision to choose the Leyland Cub as its standard one-man bus.

The prototype C 1 was the only Cub to be bodied by Chiswick but its styling set the standard for subsequent vehicles in the class. This photograph shows it after it had been fitted with a Perkins oil engine in June 1935, working on route 252A which was withdrawn in December 1936. The black roof was a feature which could be found only on the Central Bus Cubs and the 5Q5s. D.W.K. Jones

Ninety-six production buses on KPO3 chassis were eventually owned. The first seventy-four were Country Area buses with metal-framed bodywork by Short Bros. of Rochester (C 2B–75B) built in 1935 and twenty-two were Central buses, with Weymann metal-framed bodywork, built in 1936 (C 77–98). C 77–98 had a new indirect injection 4.7 litre engine, rated at 65bhp, which had been tried experimentally on C 51 in November 1935. C 51 then had more in common with the Central Bus type and was transferred from Country Buses in exchange for C 1 which itself had been fitted with a Perkins oil engine in June 1935. All were broadly similar in appearance to C 1 but had a deeper, more modern looking radiator shell and an emergency exit door in the second bay on the offside. They were finished in a striking livery which included a black roof, a feature shared only by the 5Q5s. Internally their finishings were about four years in advance of the double-deckers in having curved cappings and polished metal finishers on their window frames. There were also eight Park Royal bodied forward control 1½-deckers built in 1936 for the Inter-Station service (C 106–113) which had petrol engines and were therefore SKPZ2s. These had a large luggage compartment at the rear, with a raised passenger saloon above it and were painted in a new blue, yellow and black livery. The intervening numbers (99–105, plus 114) were allocated to eight Leyland Cub lorries (later numbered C99L etc. in the Service Vehicle fleet).

C 1 was licensed at Hounslow garage on 10th October 1934 and went into service on route 237 (Hounslow–Chertsey). It later operated from Merton and Barking. The first five production buses went into service at Northfleet on 17th April 1935 and the remainder were allocated to Dunton Green, Hertford, St Albans, Chelsham, Guildford, Leatherhead, Addlestone, Windsor, Watford, Dorking and Amersham, the last into service being C 71 at Hertford on 4th September. The Central Buses were licensed between 3rd April and 5th May 1936 and went to Mortlake, Hanwell, Enfield, Barking and Harrow Weald garages.

C 106–113 were allocated to Old Kent Road when in Inter-Station service but this facility was withdrawn on 16th September 1939 as one of the early wartime cuts. The Cubs were later put on loan to ENSA (Entertainments National Service Association). The first Cub to be withdrawn, and the only one in this period, was C 76B which was the only petrol-engined bus Cub after 1935. It was withdrawn from Windsor garage in October 1938 and sold in January 1939.

The Short Bros bodies on the 2C2s were metal-framed with radiused window pans, one of a number of details which distinguished them from the prototype C 1. Unlike their Central Bus counterparts the Country Bus Cubs did not have a route number stencil above the door, and also differed in having bumper bars. C 3 was brand new and as yet unregistered when it was photographed carrying out some kind of test which required the use the use of a mileometer on what looks like an 'arterial road'. Alan Cross

Short Bros-bodied C 72 at work in the Hertfordshire countryside while allocated to St Albans garage. The Omnibus Society

The Weymann-bodied Central Bus Cubs had a stencil route number above the offside emergency door as well as on the nearside and had no bumpers but were otherwise similar in appearance to the Short Bros version. C 94 was one of eight allocated to Enfield garage to replace Dennis Darts. A. Duke

Hinged doors in front of the rear axle on the offside and at the back of the Inter Station Cubs, gave easy access to the luggage compartment ahead of which there was an emergency exit door serving both levels. The arrows flanking the stop light were direction indicators which were operated in conjunction with semaphore signalling arms fitted in the front bulkhead pillars. This is C 107 in service at King's Cross station. R.D. and P.B. Okill

The Park Royal bodywork for the Inter Station buses was fussily variable on the nearside as the fuel tank, a sliding door and the large luggage compartment had to be accommodated within a total length of 23ft 11ins. To provide enough interior space at the lower level for seats, the arrangement of the passenger entrance was the reverse of normal, with a forward sliding door and the entrance steps against the luggage compartment bulkhead. C 108 was photographed when new, before entering service.
Capital Transport collection

Chassis:	Leyland Cub KP3 (C 1, 76); KPO3 (C 2–75, 77–98); SKPZ2 (C 106–113)
Engine:	Leyland 6-cylinder 4.4 litre 60 bhp petrol (C 1[1], 76);
	6-cylinder 4.4 litre direct injection 55 bhp oil (C 2–75[2]);
	6-cylinder 4.7 litre indirect injection 65 bhp oil (C 77–98);
	6-cylinder 4.7 litre 85 bhp overhead valve petrol (C 106–113)
Transmission:	Leyland 4-speed crash
Bodywork:	LPTB (Chiswick) (C 1); Short Bros. (C 2–75); Weymann (C 77–98);
	Park Royal (C 106–113); Unknown (C 76)
Capacity:	B20F (C 106–113 DP20F)
L.T. codes:	1C1 (C 1); 2C2 (C 2–75); 1/2C2 (77–98); 3C3 (106–113)
Built:	1932 (C 76); 1934 (C 1); 1935 (2–75); 1936 (C 77–98, 106–113)
Number built:	106
Number in stock:	1.7.33: Nil 31.12.39: 105

[1] C 1's petrol engine was replaced by a Perkins Leopard 4-cylinder oil engine in June 1935.
[2] C 55 was fitted with a 4.7 litre 65 bhp indirect injection oil engine in November 1935.

C		Date into stock		C		Date into stock	Date out of stock
1	AYV717	10.9.34		54	BXD679	21.6.35	
2	BXD631	14.3.35		55	BXD680	25.6.35	
3	BXD627	21.3.35		56	BXD681	26.6.35	
4	BXD628	25.3.35		57	BXD682	27.6.35	
5	BXD629	29.3.35		58	BXD683	27.6.35	
6	BXD632	5.4.35		59	BXD684	2.7.35	
7	BXD630	12.4.35		60	BXD685	3.7.35	
8	BXD633	15.4.35		61	BXD686	5.7.35	
9	BXD634	24.4.35		62	BXD687	10.7.35	
10	BXD635	24.4.35		63	BXD688	10.7.35	
11	BXD636	24.4.35		64	BXD689	15.7.35	
12	BXD637	2.5.35		65	BXD690	19.7.35	
13	BXD638	25.4.35		66	BXD691	19.7.35	
14	BXD639	2.5.35		67	BXD692	29.7.35	
15	BXD640	2.5.35		68	BXD693	29.7.35	
16	BXD641	7.5.35		69	BXD694	1.8.35	
17	BXD642	7.5.35		70	BXD695	1.8.35	
18	BXD643	7.5.35		71	BXD696	14.8.35	
19	BXD644	9.5.35		72	BXD697	14.8.35	
20	BXD645	9.5.35		73	BXD698	22.8.35	
21	BXD646	14.5.35		74	BXD699	22.8.35	
22	BXD647	14.5.35		75	BXD700	29.8.35	
23	BXD648	15.5.35		76	JH2401	10.11.33	31.1.39
24	BXD649	15.5.35		77	CLE105	23.3.36	
25	BXD650	20.5.35		78	CLE106	27.3.36	
26	BXD651	20.5.35		79	CLE107	27.3.36	
27	BXD652	20.5.35		80	CLE108	31.3.36	
28	BXD653	20.5.35		81	CLE109	2.4.36	
29	BXD654	22.5.35		82	CLE110	31.3.36	
30	BXD655	22.5.35		83	CLE111	2.4.36	
31	BXD656	23.5.35		84	CLE112	4.4.36	
32	BXD657	23.5.35		85	CLE113	7.4.36	
33	BXD658	24.5.35		86	CLE114	8.4.36	
34	BXD659	24.5.35		87	CLE115	16.4.36	
35	BXD660	27.5.35		88	CLE116	16.4.36	
36	BXD661	27.5.35		89	CLE117	14.4.36	
37	BXD662	30.5.35		90	CLE118	17.4.36	
38	BXD663	30.5.35		91	CLE119	16.4.36	
39	BXD664	3.6.35		92	CLE120	20.4.36	
40	BXD665	3.6.35		93	CLE121	21.4.36	
41	BXD666	3.6.35		94	CLE122	22.4.36	
42	BXD667	6.6.35		95	CLE123	24.4.36	
43	BXD668	6.6.35		96	CLE124	29.4.36	
44	BXD669	11.6.35		97	CLE125	9.5.36	
45	BXD670	11.6.35		98	CLE126	9.5.36	
46	BXD671	11.6.35		106	CLX543	10.6.36	
47	BXD672	13.6.35		107	CLX544	24.6.36	
48	BXD673	13.6.35		108	CLX545	2.7.36	
49	BXD674	17.6.35		109	CLX546	4.7.36	
50	BXD675	17.6.35		110	CLX547	9.7.36	
51	BXD676	19.6.35		111	CLX548	11.7.36	
52	BXD677	19.6.35		112	CLX549	17.7.36	
53	BXD678	21.6.35		113	CLX550	18.7.36	

Q 1 was transferred to Country Buses in February 1934 and allocated to Reigate, where it is seen after having its front end modified to resemble the 4Q4 type. In 1938 the two seats ahead of the front wheels, alongside the driver, were removed and a full-width bulkhead inserted, reducing the capacity to 35. Ken Glazier collection

Q

The AEC 'Q' was a revolutionary new design in which the engine and radiator were carried on the offside of the chassis immediately behind the front wheels, releasing the space normally occupied by the engine for extra seating. The rear axle was placed closer than usual to the back of the chassis, reducing the weight enough to allow the use of single wheels. This arrangement enabled the springs to be spaced more widely and the differential moved further to the side to enable an almost straight transmission line. The engine of Q 1 was a modified version of the 7.4 litre petrol engine used on LTs and STLs, the gearbox a conventional 'crash' unit and the brakes were vacuum-hydraulic.

The body of the prototype, numbered Q 1, was built by the LGOC at Chiswick Works to a sleek full-fronted design. Its passenger entrance was behind the front wheels and was unique for a bus in the Metropolitan area in having a sliding platform door. The interior design and finish, although rather austere, anticipated standards which were not to become common on single-deckers for at least three years, by the use of rounded window cappings. These did not become standard on double-deckers until the advent of the RT seven years later. There were originally 38 seats, compared to 30 in a conventional two-axle single-decker, but this was reduced to 37 before it entered service, two of which were alongside the driver. Q 1 was put into experimental service in September 1932, first on route 11E and then, from October, on the Nunhead circular route 621A/621B. In February 1934, after passing to London Transport, it was painted green and transferred to the Country Bus department for operation at Reigate.

London Transport's first order for large saloons was for 100 centre-entrance Qs for the Country Bus department (Q 6B–105B; coded 4Q4), to which two were added shortly afterwards (Q 186B/187B). The chassis were basically the same as Q 1 but, unlike the prototype, they had oil engines, preselective gearboxes and fluid flywheels, all specially designed to accommodate the unique anti-clockwise rotation of the engine. This specification remained standard for all of London Transport's single-deck Qs.

The ultra-modern uncluttered and well balanced lines of the Birmingham Railway Carriage & Wagon Company's bodywork for the 4Q4 were very much in keeping with the design sentiment of the LPTB and the main features are well illustrated here. The downward slope of the beading above the side windows emphasised the pronounced taper of the roof which distinguished it most obviously from other members of the class.
Capital Transport collection

The 4Q4s had Birmingham Railway Carriage & Wagon Company Ltd bodywork seating thirty-eight in a layout similar to Q 1, with two seats alongside the driver. This arrangement proved to be unsatisfactory in service because it obstructed the driver's view to the nearside, which was already impaired by the full-width front. Between March and October 1936 these seats were removed and a full-width bulkhead was installed, access to the driver's cab being provided through a hinged door in the centre. These modifications reduced the seating capacity to 35. Q 186B and 187B had this arrangement when they were built. Interior finish included rounded pillar shrouds and polished cappings and the brown, green and cream colour scheme recently introduced on the STL class. Externally, they were instantly recognisable by the downward slope of the roof from front to back which appeared more pronounced on these bodies because the roof guttering followed the same profile.

Q 8B, was licensed at Watford High Street garage on 6th July 1935 and the remainder of the first hundred were in service by January 1936 at a total of 15 garages, where they replaced ADC, Thornycroft and Tilling-Stevens vehicles.

The first London Transport saloons for Central buses were 80 Qs with a shorter wheelbase so that a doorless entrance could be placed ahead of the front axle (Q 106–185; 5Q5). Their bodywork was by Park Royal who produced a neater design with wider pillar spacing and guttering which followed the line of the windows. The emergency door was removed to the rear wall, further improving the appearance of the offside, which was rather cluttered on the BRCW bodies. These were the only buses, apart from the Central Bus Cubs which had black roofs but this lasted only until the first overhaul when it was replaced by the standard grey. The 37 seats were arranged in 14 forward facing doubles, with longitudinal seats over the engine compartment and front wheels. The transverse seats had tubular frames and the interior design was an improved version of the 4Q4 with a neater finish to the window shrouds. They were also fitted with wind-down opening windows, three on each side, the operating handles being placed centrally at the top of the frame. The layout and overall appearance was very similar to that adopted for the RF class fifteen years later.

Only 53 were red, because the last 27 to be built were diverted to the Country Bus department to release a like number of 4Q4s for use as Green Line coaches (see fleet list). The first four (Q 108, 110, 112 and 115) were licensed at Merton and Dalston on 4th March 1936, and later deliveries went to Chalk Farm, Old Kent Road and Merton, directly or indirectly replacing the DE, LN and S classes, starting up new routes or being used to upgrade routes from one-man operation. The Country Bus 5Q5s went at first to Reigate, Amersham, Two Waters, Northfleet, Hatfield and Hertford garages but were later concentrated at Dorking, Guildford, Hatfield and Hertford. Q 181B, 183B–185B were transferred to Central Buses and repainted red in October 1938.

Unfortunately, the offside of the 4Q4 was not so harmonious as the nearside because the position of the emergency exit door and the presence of the engine upset the balance. Because the front axle was set back slightly, the driver's cab door was over the wheel and swung towards the back, obliging the driver to enter the cab wrong-footed. These were buses but Reigate's Q 11B is doing a turn on Green Line route J. These were the only motor bus bodies supplied by BRCW to London Transport, although they did build 390 trolleybuses. A.N. Porter

The 5Q5 was the only version of the Q successfully to take maximum advantage of the high passenger capacity made possible by the side-engine. Being designed for Central Bus operation, it was caught by the restrictions imposed by the Metropolitan Police and there was therefore no requirement for a sliding platform door. This enabled the entrance to go ahead of the front axle, leaving the whole of the saloon available for passengers, for whom 37 seats were provided, seven more than a conventional bus of the period. Q 171B, one of the 27 which were painted green, is at Hertford on route 341, whose operation it shared with a 4Q4 from Hertford garage. J.F. Higham

This rear view of Q 120, in the red livery worn by the majority, shows how much more successful Park Royal had been in producing a neat and tidy offside design, with the help of the shorter wheelbase. This was done primarily by removing the emergency door to the rear wall at the expense of one seat, which cleared the way for the number of bays to be reduced to five and the side windows lengthened. The rear overhang on the Q was shorter than on other types and the better weight distribution allowed the use of single tyres on the rear wheels. The photograph was taken at the Lower Morden terminus of route 225 which received Qs in place of DA-type omo buses in April 1936. London's Transport Museum

The last 50 Qs were also by Park Royal but were long wheelbase 32 seat centre entrance Green Line coaches with full-width drivers' cabs (Q 189c–238c; 6Q6). In line with Country Bus policy, these reverted to having a door immediately behind the front wheels but in most respects were similar in design to the 5Q5s. On this batch, the sloping roof was abandoned which, combined with the higher floor line also adopted on the 5Q5s and a deeper roof, gave the completed vehicle a taller less elongated appearance. Internally they were finished to full Green Line standards, with a saloon heater, deeper seat cushions, ash trays on moquette-covered seat backs, and luggage racks above the seats. The first complete vehicle (Q 189c) was received at Chiswick on 25th September 1936, the first to be licensed was Q 197c at Guildford on 3rd November 1936 and all 50 were in service by 21st January 1937. Between them Guildford and Hertford received the bulk of the class, with smaller numbers going to Addlestone, Luton, Amersham and High Wycombe.

The 27 4Q4s released by the 5Q5s (Q 81–105, 186, 187) were delicensed on 1st October 1936 to be made ready for Green Line service. Before this happened, seven were painted red and placed on loan to Central Buses in November (Q 101–105, to Cricklewood for route 226) or December (Q 186, 187, to Kingston) to cover a temporary shortage of large saloons in that department. They all returned to Country Bus stock on 1st March 1937 and joined the others at Chiswick for modification. The alterations carried out were limited to the essentials of painting them in Green Line colours, fitting them with saloon heaters, luggage racks and external brackets to carry route boards and putting a dummy radiator grille on the front. Their rather spartan wooden-framed bus seats were not changed. They were reclassified 1/4Q4/1. They were added to the Green Line fleet so that the remaining Gilfords could be withdrawn from coach service and were allocated to Amersham, Leatherhead, Northfleet and Staines from 27th March 1937. They remained on Green Line service until August or September 1938, when they were replaced by the new 10T10s and reverted to bus work. They had their saloon heaters removed but were otherwise unchanged and retained their revised coding.

In common with all Green Line coaches, the 6Q6s were converted to public ambulances on 1st September 1939 owing to the imminent outbreak of the Second World War.

There were also five double-deck Qs.

The Green Line Qs needed a sliding door behind the front axle and therefore reverted to the longer (18ft 6ins) wheelbase version of the chassis with its shorter front overhang. The metal-framed Park Royal bodies were also significantly taller, at 9ft 11ins, because they had a higher saloon floor so that as many seats as possible could face forward. They were built with full width cabs, limiting their capacity to an uninspiring 32 seats and enforcing the inclusion of a driver's cab door. The straight roofline helped to give the main body section a handsome aspect but the front was a disappointment. The rectangular grille served no practical purpose and failed to match the quality of design of the rest of the vehicle while the use of flat panelling robbed it of any sense of style. Q 195c was photographed at Chiswick before entering service. London's Transport Museum

The 5Q5 pre-dated the RF by 15 years but the interior was remarkably similar in appearance. Eighty of this design were purchased in 1936 for Central Area work.
Alan Townsin collection

Chassis:	AEC 'Q' 762 (Q 1); 0762 (remainder)
Engine:	AEC A167 6-cylinder 7.4 litre 95 bhp petrol (Q 1)
	AEC A170 6-cylinder 7.7 litre 95 bhp oil (remainder)
Transmission:	AEC 4-speed crash (Q 1); AEC D133 4-speed direct selection preselective with fluid flywheel (remainder)
Bodywork:	LGOC (Chiswick) (Q 1); Birmingham Railway Carriage & Wagon Co. Ltd (Q 6–105, 186, 187); Park Royal (remainder).
Capacity:	B35C[1] (Q 1, 6–105, 186, 187); B37F (Q 106–185); DP32C (Q 189–238)
L.T. code:	1Q1 (Q 1); 4Q4[2] (6–105, 186, 187); 5Q5 (106–185); 6Q6 (189–238)
Built:	1932 (Q 1); 1935/1936 (4Q4); 1936 (5Q5); 1936/1937 (6Q6).
Number built:	233

Number in stock: 1.7.33: 1; 31.12.39: 233

[1] Q 1 and 6–105 were originally B37C but were converted to B35C in September 1938 (Q 1) or between March and October 1936 (remainder).
[2] Q 81–105, 186, 187 were converted for Green Line operation in 1936/1937 and reclassified 1/4Q4/1

Q		Date into stock	Q		Date into stock	Q		Date into stock
1	GX5395	1.7.33	16	BXD537	12.7.35	27	BXD548	30.7.35
6	BXD527	23.5.35	17	BXD538	16.7.35	28	BXD549	30.7.35
7	BXD528	25.6.35	18	BXD539	17.7.35	29	BXD550	1.8.35
8	BXD529	27.6.35	19	BXD541	18.7.35	30	BXD551	1.8.35
9	BXD530	3.7.35	20	BXD540	18.7.35	31	BXD552	13.8.35
10	BXD531	3.7.35	21	BXD542	23.7.35	32	BXD553	13.8.35
11	BXD532	8.7.35	22	BXD543	23.7.35	33	BXD554	13.8.35
12	BXD533	8.7.35	23	BXD544	29.7.35	34	BXD555	15.8.35
13	BXD534	10.7.35	24	BXD545	29.7.35	35	BXD556	15.8.35
14	BXD535	10.7.35	25	BXD546	29.7.35	36	BXD557	21.8.35
15	BXD536	12.7.35	26	BXD547	30.7.35	37	BXD558	21.8.35

Q		Date into stock	Q		Date into stock	Q		Date into stock
38	BXD559	21.8.35	105	CGJ210	6.12.35	g 172	CLE195	25.6.36
39	BXD560	22.8.35	106	CLE129	4.3.36	g 173	CLE196	10.8.36
40	BXD561	22.8.35	107	CLE130	6.3.36	g 174	CLE197	24.7.36
41	BXD562	27.8.35	108	CLE131	25.2.36	g 175	CLE198	17.8.36
42	BXD563	27.8.35	109	CLE132	3.2.36	g 176	CLE199	17.7.36
43	BXD564	29.8.35	110	CLE133	28.2.36	g 177	CLE200	20.8.36
44	BXD565	29.8.35	111	CLE134	27.2.36	g 178	CLE201	13.7.36
45	BXD566	29.8.35	112	CLE135	27.2.36	g 179	CLE202	22.7.36
46	BXD567	3.9.35	113	CLE136	8.4.36	g 180	CLE203	1.8.36
47	BXD568	3.9.35	114	CLE137	11.3.36	g 181	CLE204	26.8.36
48	BXD569	3.9.35	115	CLE138	29.2.36	g 182	CLE205	18.8.36
49	BXD570	5.9.35	116	CLE139	15.4.36	g 183	CLE206	21.8.36
50	BXD571	7.9.35	117	CLE140	5.3.36	g 184	CLE207	28.8.36
51	BXD572	10.9.35	118	CLE141	12.3.36	g 185	CLE208	26.8.36
52	BXD573	10.9.35	119	CLE142	23.3.36	186	CLE127	15.6.36
53	BXD574	12.9.35	120	CLE143	17.4.36	187	CLE128	15.6.36
54	BXD575	12.9.35	121	CLE144	22.4.36	189	CXX382	25.9.36
55	BXD576	12.9.35	122	CLE145	10.3.36	190	CXX383	2.11.36
56	CGJ161	17.9.35	123	CLE146	23.3.36	191	CXX384	3.11.36
57	CGJ162	17.9.35	124	CLE147	19.3.36	192	CXX385	17.11.36
58	CGJ163	19.9.35	125	CLE148	8.5.36	193	CXX386	30.10.36
59	CGJ164	19.9.35	126	CLE149	30.4.36	194	CXX387	6.11.36
60	CGJ165	19.9.35	127	CLE150	26.3.36	195	CXX388	9.11.36
61	CGJ166	24.9.35	128	CLE151	29.4.36	196	CXX389	30.10.36
62	CGJ167	24.9.35	129	CLE152	4.4.36	197	CXX390	21.10.36
63	CGJ168	26.9.35	130	CLE153	25.3.36	198	CXX391	24.10.36
64	CGJ169	26.9.35	131	CLE154	7.3.36	199	CXX392	17.11.36
65	CGJ170	26.9.35	132	CLE155	18.3.36	200	CXX393	12.10.36
66	CGJ171	1.10.35	133	CLE156	6.5.36	201	CXX394	3.12.36
67	CGJ172	1.10.35	134	CLE157	31.3.36	202	CXX395	17.11.36
68	CGJ173	3.10.35	135	CLE158	4.5.36	203	CXX396	22.10.36
69	CGJ174	3.10.35	136	CLE159	12.5.36	204	CXX397	27.10.36
70	CGJ175	3.10.35	137	CLE160	31.3.36	205	CXX398	1.12.36
71	CGJ176	8.10.35	138	CLE161	14.3.36	206	CXX399	21.10.36
72	CGJ177	8.10.35	139	CLE162	20.4.36	207	CXX400	20.11.36
73	CGJ178	10.10.35	140	CLE163	15.5.36	208	CXX401	1.12.36
74	CGJ179	10.10.35	141	CLE164	27.4.36	209	CXX402	12.11.36
75	CGJ180	10.10.35	142	CLE165	14.5.36	210	CXX403	3.12.36
76	CGJ181	15.10.35	143	CLE166	8.5.36	211	CXX404	28.11.36
77	CGJ182	15.10.35	144	CLE167	24.4.36	212	CXX405	25.11.36
78	CGJ183	17.10.35	145	CLE168	8.4.36	213	CXX406	19.12.36
79	CGJ184	17.10.35	146	CLE169	14.5.36	214	DGX220	23.11.36
80	CGJ185	17.10.35	147	CLE170	21.4.36	215	DGX221	7.12.36
81	CGJ186	22.10.35	148	CLE171	31.3.36	216	DGX222	9.12.36
82	CGJ187	22.10.35	149	CLE172	27.5.36	217	DGX223	28.11.36
83	CGJ188	24.10.35	150	CLE173	30.4.36	218	DGX224	19.11.36
84	CGJ189	24.10.35	g 151	CLE174	16.6.36	219	DGX225	21.11.36
85	CGJ190	24.10.35	g 152	CLE175	1.9.36	220	DGX226	24.11.36
86	CGJ191	29.10.35	153	CLE176	19.5.36	221	DGX227	9.12.36
87	CGJ192	29.10.35	154	CLE177	23.5.36	222	DGX228	10.11.36
88	CGJ193	31.10.35	g 155	CLE178	11.6.36	223	DGX229	28.11.36
89	CGJ195	1.11.35	156	CLE179	25.5.36	224	DGX230	22.12.36
90	CGJ194	31.10.35	157	CLE180	18.5.36	225	DGX231	11.12.36
91	CGJ196	5.11.35	158	CLE181	26.5.36	226	DGX232	22.12.36
92	CGJ197	8.11.35	g 159	CLE182	15.6.36	227	DGX233	10.12.36
93	CGJ198	8.11.35	160	CLE183	5.6.36	228	DGX234	5.12.36
94	CGJ199	8.11.35	161	CLE184	21.5.36	229	DGX235	17.12.36
95	CGJ200	8.11.35	g 162	CLE185	30.6.36	230	DGX236	18.12.36
96	CGJ201	13.11.35	g 163	CLE186	12.6.36	231	DGX237	15.10.36
97	CGJ202	13.11.35	g 164	CLE187	13.6.36	232	DGX238	15.12.36
98	CGJ203	19.11.35	165	CLE188	29.5.36	233	DGX239	10.12.36
99	CGJ204	19.11.35	g 166	CLE189	23.6.36	234	DGX240	30.12.36
100	CGJ205	21.11.35	g 167	CLE190	17.6.36	235	DGX241	4.1.37
101	CGJ206	21.11.35	g 168	CLE191	25.6.36	236	DGX242	30.12.36
102	CGJ207	28.11.35	g 169	CLE192	23.7.36	237	DGX243	7.1.37
103	CGJ208	28.11.35	g 170	CLE193	14.8.36	238	DGX244	5.1.37
104	CGJ209	6.12.35	g 171	CLE194	2.7.36			

g – Delivered in green Country Bus livery (all 4Q4 and 6Q6 were green when new).

The Weymann bodywork of the Renown coaches continued the design theme started by the 9T9s (complete with bumper bar) but without the built-up wing assembly. The opening roof section and the raffish curved rear mudguards are clearly visible in this photograph of LTC 23 at Chessington Zoo and it is also possible to see the high-backed coach seats silhouetted in the saloon windows. These were the first coaches not to carry the 'GREEN LINE' name nor a 'c' suffix to the fleet number, reflecting the transfer of responsibility for the Private Hire department to Central Buses at the end of 1937. A.N. Porter

LTC

The LTC class was purchased in 1937 to replace the life expired fleet of Private Hire coaches, mainly T class AEC Regals. The AEC Renown three-axle chassis was chosen in order to reduce wheel arch intrusion in the saloon and the mechanical specification included preselective gearboxes, fluid flywheels and petrol engines for quiet running. The engines were not new but were recovered from LT type double-deckers which received new oil engines instead. The LTCs differed from the LT class in having fully floating rear axles, which altered the appearance of the rear wheel hubs. The short-wheelbase 663 model was specified so that they could be operated with as little physical restriction as possible but the Construction & Use Regulations limited their overall length to twenty-seven feet, which made them shorter than the two-axle 9T9s whose wheelbase was greater.

Their Weymann thirty-seat bodywork was similar to the 9T9 but did not have a rear destination indicator, nor a built-up bonnet and wing assembly. Other differences included deep rear mudguards, which sloped downwards towards the rear, echoing the line of the windows and a straight cantrail moulding, omitting the upsweep which was needed on Green Line coaches to clear the side route boards. They were also fitted with sliding roof, radio and individual coach seats arranged in staggered pairs.

The first five went into service at Brixton Private Hire garage in November 1937 but the whole fleet moved to Old Kent Road when the responsibility for the Private Hire fleet was transferred from Country to Central Buses on 22nd December 1937.

On the outbreak of war in September 1939, the LTCs were converted to public ambulances.

Chassis:	AEC Renown 663		
Engine:	AEC A145 7.4 litre 95 bhp petrol		
Transmission:	AEC D132 4-speed direct acting preselective with fluid flywheel.		
Bodywork:	Weymann	Built:	1937/1938
Capacity:	C30F	Number built:	24
L.T. code:	1LTC1	Number in stock: 1.7.33: Nil	31.12.39: 24.

LTC		Date into stock	LTC		Date into stock	LTC		Date into stock
1	EGO505	8.11.37	9	EGO513	12.1.38	17	EGO521	1.2.38
2	EGO506	22.9.37	10	EGO514	3.2.38	18	EGO522	10.12.37
3	EGO507	30.9.37	11	EGO515	13.10.37	19	EGO523	11.12.37
4	EGO508	17.1.38	12	EGO516	13.11.37	20	EGO524	18.12.37
5	EGO509	21.12.37	13	EGO517	8.12.37	21	EGO525	24.12.37
6	EGO510	20.11.37	14	EGO518	5.1.38	22	EGO526	14.1.38
7	EGO511	27.1.38	15	EGO519	8.12.37	23	EGO527	4.2.38
8	EGO512	26.10.37	16	EGO520	20.1.38	24	EGO528	22.1.38

CR 1B arrives at 55 Broadway on 8th January 1938 for inspection by the Board accompanied by a C, presumably for comparison. The styling, with its downward-curving windows and voluptuously rounded and bulbous mudguards was very much in the exuberant style of the period. Unlike its contemporary TF 1, however, it had a conventional cab and canopy. D.W.K. Jones

CR

The CR was based on the REC, a revolutionary new version of the Cub chassis designed by Leyland in conjunction with London Transport, in which the standard Leyland direct injection 4.4 litre oil engine was mounted vertically at the rear in line with the chassis. The radiator and the constant-mesh gearbox, which was integrated with the rear axle, were also at the back. The twenty-seat bodywork of CR 1B, built by the LPTB at Chiswick Works, was based on the Board's contemporary standards of design and interior finish, with a distinctive downward slope to the side windows at both back and front. A half-cab layout was adopted, with the passenger doorway immediately behind the front wheels, the area above the nearside wheel not being used. The passenger entrance was fitted with a sliding door and access to the driver's cab was through an angled doorless opening from the passenger saloon. The engine compartment was inside the body and was fitted up as a luggage rack. All seats were forward-facing doubles of the latest tubular-framed variety and there was an emergency exit door in the fourth offside bay.

The production CR was a neater version of the prototype, with a straight rather than stepped section at the back and without the downward curve of the window. This allowed the roof to be deeper and visually more satisfying. The side windows were also more neatly arranged because the fuel filler was moved forward so allowing the emergency exit door to be repositioned. The front was redesigned to be part of the cab and wing structure so that the headlamps could be set lower and a smoother curve introduced onto the wheel arch. CR 9 entered service at Kingston in October 1939. London's Transport Museum

The chassis of CR 1 was delivered to Chiswick on 16th October 1937 and received its body on 31st December, the chassis meanwhile being returned to Leyland, presumably for some adjustments, between 17th and 22nd December. It was licensed in January 1938 and went to St Albans for trial operation, which was successful enough for an order for seventy-three more to be contemplated. This high figure was probably an error of calculation as the number needed to replace the remaining Bedfords and Dennis Darts fell far short of that total and was still falling as more routes were converted to larger two-man vehicles. When the order was placed it was reduced to fifty-nine, which included CR 1, but even this was still rather in excess of what was needed and was soon reduced again, to forty-nine. (This change had nothing to do with the outbreak of war as has been reported elsewhere, the cancellation having been made some time before that.) CR 2–49 had the larger 4.7-litre indirect-injection engine but were otherwise mechanically the same as the prototype. Their Chiswick-built bodies were generally similar to CR 1, but their rear domes had a less pronounced curvature and the lower line of the side windows was straight, with a shorter downward curve at the front. This enabled an extra full-width window to be included, giving a neater, less fussy appearance.

The chassis of CR 2 arrived at Chiswick on 19th July 1939, appeared as a complete bus on 8th September, after the outbreak of war, and was licensed, with CR 3, on 9th September at Kingston garage. The remaining Central buses licensed in 1939 went to Hounslow, Uxbridge and Enfield to replace the surviving buses in the DA class. CR 12B–17B were painted green and went to Windsor, replacing Cubs which then indirectly replaced the remaining Bedfords.

Chassis:	Leyland REC
Engine:	Leyland 6-cylinder: 4.4 litre direct-injection, 55 bhp oil (CR 1); 4.7 litre indirect injection 65 bhp oil, mounted vertically, in line (CR 2–46).
Transmission:	Leyland 4-speed constant mesh (helical third gear)
Bodywork:	LPTB
Capacity:	B20F
L.T. code:	1CR1 (CR 1); 2CR2 (CR 2–46)
Built:	1937 (CR 1); 1939 (CR 2–46)
Number built (by 31.12.39):	46
Number in stock:	1.7.33: Nil 31.12.39: 46

CR		Date into stock	CR		Date into stock	CR		Date into stock
1	ELP294	31.12.37	17	FXT123	30.9.39	33	FXT139	27.10.39
2	FXT108	8.9.39	18	FXT124	4.10.39	34	FXT140	28.10.39
3	FXT109	8.9.39	19	FXT125	4.10.39	35	FXT141	3.11.39
4	FXT110	14.9.39	20	FXT126	5.10.39	36	FXT142	23.11.39
5	FXT111	14.9.39	21	FXT127	7.10.39	37	FXT143	9.11.39
6	FXT112	18.9.39	22	FXT128	10.10.39	38	FXT144	10.11.39
7	FXT113	19.9.39	23	FXT129	9.10.39	39	FXT145	23.11.39
8	FXT114	19.9.39	24	FXT130	11.10.39	40	FXT146	22.11.39
9	FXT115	20.9.39	25	FXT131	14.10.39	41	FXT147	28.11.39
10	FXT116	22.9.39	26	FXT132	17.10.39	42	FXT148	1.12.39
11	FXT117	22.9.39	27	FXT133	19.10.39	43	FXT149	2.12.39
12	FXT118	26.9.39	28	FXT134	20.10.39	44	FXT150	5.12.39
13	FXT119	26.9.39	29	FXT135	21.10.39	45	FXT151	9.12.39
14	FXT120	28.9.39	30	FXT136	24.10.39	46	FXT152	21.12.39
15	FXT121	29.9.39	31	FXT137	23.10.39			
16	FXT122	2.10.39	32	FXT138	26.10.39			

TF

In 1937 London Transport and Leyland Motors Ltd co-operated in two important experiments with different positions for the engine, the first being the TF which had its engine under the floor for the first time. The new Leyland chassis, which was designated FEC had an 8.6 litre 94 bhp engine, modified for mounting horizontally on the offside of the chassis behind the front axle. Unusually for a Leyland, the TF had a preselective gearbox, supplied by AEC, operating through a fluid flywheel. The gears and brakes, were air-operated, both new developments on a London motor bus. The selector was of the electro-magnetic type mounted on the steering column but this was later replaced by a standard floor-mounted gear stick, as used on STL and other contemporary types. The radiator was mounted vertically at the front. The prototype TF 1C had a Leyland body which was similar in many respects to the contemporary Chiswick designs but with swept down front and rear saloon windows and streamlined mudguards. As originally built, TF 1C had an exceptionally high driving position giving the driver an incomparable all-round view through an idiosyncratic windscreen which ran from waist level almost to the top of the roof, giving the impression of a glasshouse. To allow the inclusion of a sliding door, the entrance was behind the front axle and the area ahead of the nearside bulkhead was effectually a wide wing. The 34 seats were arranged in forward facing pairs, with one double seat in front of the entrance on the nearside. Access to the driver's cab was from the passenger saloon.

TF 1C was delivered to London Transport on 19th July 1937 but then spent five months under the care of the engineering department before being licensed at Tunbridge Wells garage for service on routes C1 and C2 (Tunbridge Wells–Chertsey/ Woking) on 1st December. It was later transferred to Romford (London Road) garage.

There were two production batches: 12 Private Hire coaches (TF 2C–13C) with Park Royal 33-seat bodywork; and 75 Green Line coaches with LPTB (Chiswick) 34-seat bodywork (TF 14C–88C). The basic layout was the same as on TF 1 but significant changes included a more conventional driving position and cab, a straight window line and the incorporation of a radiator grille and filler cap in the nearside wing. The Private Hire coaches also differed in having glass cant panels for sightseeing, a sliding roof, radio, an offside emergency exit and no rear destination indicator. All TFs had a higher floor line with three steps up from the kerb. The interior finish of the Green Line version was similar to the 10T10s, including the last examples of window winders placed centrally above the saloon windows.

The first completed production coach was Green Line TF 14C which was ready on 2nd February 1939 and the first Private Hire vehicle, TF 2C, was received from Park Royal on 29th March. Delivery of the Private Hire coaches was completed on 9th June with the delivery of TF 12C, which had been earmarked as the Directors' coach and had its seating reduced to 25. All were allocated to Old Kent Road garage, the private hire base. The Green Line TFs all went to Romford (London Road) for the busy East End coach routes, delivery being completed in August 1939. TF 14C was used as a trainer between 2nd February and 24th March 1939, after which its body was removed and the chassis returned to Leyland for reasons unknown. Its original body, number 1 in the new series started with the TFs, was mounted on TF 75C and it received a new body on 5th August but it was not licensed until the fateful 1st September. The last to be completed was TF 76C, on 21st August, but it was not licensed until 15th September by when it was converted to an ambulance.

The TFs saw little service before the war as, in common with all Green Line coaches, they were withdrawn for use as public ambulances on the outbreak of war. The Private Hire coaches were used as Country Buses for a time but were delicensed in November 1939.

Both chassis and body of underfloor-engined TF 1c were built by Leyland to the specification of London Transport but the cab, in which the driver can be seen sitting high up above waist level, was unlike anything designed before or since at Chiswick. The destination blind box was also non-standard but in other respects it was similar to the contemporary CR 1, although the flared skirt panels were unique to this coach. Like the 6Q6s, the design did not realise the full capacity potential of the uninterrupted floor space because a sliding door had to be installed behind the front axle and the space above the front wheel was wasted. D.W.K. Jones

It is not known when TF 1c had its cab and front dome modified to this more conventional arrangement but the fact that it is dressed for the C1 suggests it was some time before its reallocation to Romford and therefore probably at first overhaul. The front bulkhead did not blend so neatly with the wing on the prototype as it did on production coaches and the wing itself was set much lower. The TFs had a higher floor than the Regals with three, rather than two, steps up into the saloon, as can be seen through the open doorway.
Alan Cross

The Park Royal bodies of the sightseeing TFs were broadly similar in basic design to the Green Line version but, as can be seen here, had glass cant panels and an opening roof which in combination almost completely opened the saloon to sunshine and daylight. A rather ungainly radio aerial sits on the front dome of TF 9c above the single line blind which was considered sufficient for the needs of the type of service on which it was to be used. London's Transport Museum

The Green Line TFs had a straight waistline but were otherwise similar in style to the 10T10 coaches which had preceded them. They were finished in a new livery of Lincoln green on the main body panels with a light green relief around the windows. This vehicle was wrongly numbered TF 2c by the licensing office at Chiswick but this was corrected to TF 14c before it entered service. At the time of the photograph it carried body number 1 in the new series which started with the TFs. Alan Cross

The entire batch of 2TF3s was allocated to Romford (London Road) for the high frequency coach services X, Y1 and Y2. They saw little service before being withdrawn at short notice on 1st September 1939 for conversion to public ambulances and were therefore little photographed in their original condition. TF 60c is parked on layover in the Minories lay-by at Aldgate soon after it entered service in May 1939.
G. Robbins collection

Chassis: Leyland Tiger FEC
Engine: Leyland 8.6 litre direct injection 94 bhp oil, horizontal.
Transmission: AEC D132 air-operated direct selection preselective with fluid flywheel.
Bodywork: Leyland (TF 1); Park Royal (TF 2–13); LPTB (TF 14–88)
Capacity: DP34F (TF 14–88); C33F (TF 2–11); C25F (TF 12).
L.T. code: 1TF1 (TF 1); 2TF2 (TF 2–13); 2TF3 (TF 14–88)
Built: 1937 (TF1); 1939 (TF 2–88)
Number built: 88
Number in stock: 1.7.33: Nil   31.12.39: 88

TF		Date into stock	TF		Date into stock	TF		Date into stock
1	DYL904	10.7.37	31	FJJ642	29.3.39	61	FJJ672	10.5.39
2	FJJ603	29.3.39	32	FJJ643	13.4.39	62	FJJ673	6.5.39
3	FJJ604	31.3.39	33	FJJ644	1.4.39	63	FJJ674	15.5.39
4	FJJ605	6.5.39	34	FJJ645	28.3.39	64	FJJ761	19.5.39
5	FJJ606	6.5.39	35	FJJ646	31.3.39	65	FJJ762	30.5.39
6	FJJ607	15.5.39	36	FJJ647	5.4.39	66	FJJ763	17.5.39
7	FJJ608	31.3.39	37	FJJ648	6.4.39	67	FJJ764	20.5.39
8	FJJ609	4.4.39	38	FJJ649	30.3.39	68	FJJ765	22.5.39
9	FJJ610	3.4.39	39	FJJ650	4.4.39	69	FJJ766	25.5.39
10	FJJ611	5.4.39	40	FJJ651	4.4.39	70	FJJ767	26.5.39
11	FJJ612	28.4.39	41	FJJ652	12.4.39	71	FJJ768	5.6.39
12	FJJ613	9.6.39	42	FJJ653	11.4.39	72	FJJ769	24.5.39
13	FJJ614	28.4.39	43	FJJ654	18.4.39	73	FJJ770	2.6.39
14	FJJ615	2.2.39	44	FJJ655	19.4.39	74	FJJ771	1.6.39
15	FJJ616	13.2.39	45	FJJ656	24.4.39	75	FJJ772	31.5.39
16	FJJ617	21.2.39	46	FJJ657	12.4.39	76	FJJ773	21.8.39
17	FJJ618	16.2.39	47	FJJ658	14.4.39	77	FJJ774	6.6.39
18	FJJ629	10.3.39	48	FJJ659	21.4.39	78	FJJ775	8.6.39
19	FJJ630	18.3.39	49	FJJ660	28.4.39	79	FJJ776	16.6.39
20	FJJ631	10.3.39	50	FJJ661	20.4.39	80	FJJ777	19.6.39
21	FJJ632	10.3.39	51	FJJ662	24.4.39	81	FXT41	20.6.39
22	FJJ633	13.3.39	52	FJJ663	25.4.39	82	FXT42	22.6.39
23	FJJ634	14.3.39	53	FJJ664	29.4.39	83	FXT43	28.6.39
24	FJJ635	17.3.39	54	FJJ665	27.4.39	84	FXT44	4.8.39
25	FJJ636	21.3.39	55	FJJ666	2.5.39	85	FXT45	6.7.39
26	FJJ637	20.3.39	56	FJJ667	3.5.39	86	FXT46	29.7.39
27	FJJ638	23.3.39	57	FJJ668	5.5.39	87	FXT47	27.7.39
28	FJJ639	22.3.39	58	FJJ669	10.5.39	88	FXT48	3.8.39
29	FJJ640	24.3.39	59	FJJ670	11.5.39			
30	FJJ641	25.3.39	60	FJJ671	12.5.39			

These drawings were submitted by Brush Electrical Engineering to accompany their tender to build the bodies for twelve private hire TF coaches. There are interesting differences from the Park Royal design eventually chosen but there is a basic common theme which suggests a fairly tight specification. London's Transport Museum

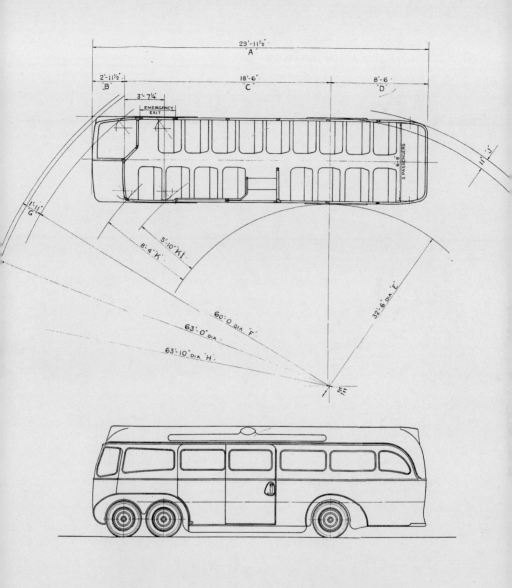

In 1939 London Transport sought authority to operate a 30ft coach experimentally on Green Line route A1. This drawing was submitted with the application and is clearly a twin-steer version of the TF, an arrangement chosen because of its excellent turning circle, which it was hoped would meet the limits imposed by the Metropolitan Police. None was built, but Leyland did produce a single prototype chassis, known as the Panda, which could probably have been used for the London experiment. Public Record Office

MINOR TYPES

The following lists show the single-deckers acquired from Independents either by the LGOC and associated companies before 1933 or directly by the LPTB which did not fit into any of the larger classes. It is therefore presented in a condensed form which lists the details separately under individual headings for each chassis make, arranged alphabetically.

The lists under each heading are arranged in numerical order of fleet numbers, where these were allocated. Those vehicles remaining unnumbered until withdrawn are shown at the end of each list, in most cases in alphabetical and numerical order of the registration numbers.

The Albion PKB 26 was introduced in 1930 and had a six-cylinder petrol engine with an output of 60 bhp. UV5761 had been a coach in the fleet of the Lewis Bus Company of Watford but during its short career with London Transport it was used as a bus. When photographed in Market Street Watford it was wearing the first, green and black, Country Bus colour scheme and the GENERAL fleet name. D.W.K. Jones

The PM28 was Albion's first forward-control single-deck model, introduced in 1927 and had a 60 bhp petrol engine and a wheelbase of 16ft. The rather austere looking 32-seat body on CH7935 was built by the London Midland and Scottish Railway who had run it on services in the Tring and Boxmoor areas before they were taken over by LGCS in April 1933. In London Transport ownership it continued to run in the same areas. J.F. Higham

The only Albion which stayed long enough to receive a fleet number was AN 1c, which was acquired from Sunset Pullman Coaches and later joined the Private Hire fleet. Its Duple 31-seat body was mounted on a Valkyrie PV70 chassis, a model introduced in 1933 which had a four-cylinder 6.1 litre petrol engine, an improvement on the original 5 litre Valkyrie of 1930. It remained in the fleet until the arrival of the 10T10s in March 1938. D.W.K. Jones

British Associated Transport was a short-lived manufacturer based in Bristol who produced two versions of the Cruiser, UR8310 being one of the 20-seat version with a 6-cylinder engine. This bus was unique in the LPTB fleet and was withdrawn almost immediately after it was taken into stock. It is seen here stored awaiting disposal, still in St Albans & District colours.
Ken Glazier collection

The Bristol B, also known as the Superbus, was introduced in October 1926 and had a four-cylinder side-valve engine of 5.99 litre capacity, developing 75bhp at 2,000 rpm. London Transport acquired four, all from the Lewis company of Watford, two coaches and, as here, two Strachan-bodied 32-seat buses. UR3832, still on home ground in Market Street Watford, lasted less than two years with the Board, its non-standard status overwhelming its undoubted qualities as a bus.
J.F. Higham

The Bean chassis had a brief period of popularity in the years before the LPTB was formed and there were thirteen owned by companies acquired by the Board, five of which went into the Central Bus fleet and therefore had fleet numbers. BN 1 was one of four which came from the LGOC who had bought them with the businesses of Royal Highlander (BN 1–3) and Pinner Bus (BN 4). The Birch 14-seat bodywork on the Royal Highlander buses was only 6ft 6in wide as they were designed to operate on route 211 which had some width restrictions in West Ealing. BN 1 is loading outside the District Line station at **Ealing Broadway.** Ken Glazier collection

GJ5077 with its neat little Willowbrook 14-seat body, was first owned by Sevenoaks & District but passed to East Surrey with that business in 1931 and eventually to LGCS. London Transport wasted little time in withdrawing it, although it was in service long enough to be repainted into Country Bus green and black. It is parked in Reigate garage after withdrawal with a similarly fated NS in the background. H.J. Snook/Ken Glazier collection

The Chevrolet Motor Co. was owned by General Motors and produced a range of 14-seat models in the 1920s, forerunners of the highly successful Bedford range. The Chevrolet U was the 1930 version and the last to be launched before the Bedford company was formed. KX6513 was an Amersham & District bus but, like many acquired small buses, was quickly withdrawn by the LPTB and found a new home for a while in the Isle of Lewis. D.W.K. Jones

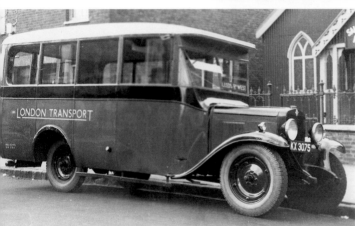

This Chevrolet LQ formerly owned by Bell's Bus Service of Slough survived long enough, still operating in Slough, to be given a LONDON TRANSPORT fleet name but was withdrawn soon after. J.F. Higham

Although the builders of the bodies on most of the Chevrolets is not known, the design of those illustrated differed from each other in many ways and in this case most strikingly. PG9110 came from The Egham Motor Co. who bought it in 1930 but, even though it was given a repaint, its life with London Transport lasted barely seven months. The Omnibus Society/J.F. Higham

Six Weymann-bodied Commer Invader coaches were bought for East Surrey in 1931 as Private Hire coaches but ended their days with London Transport as 18-seat buses. GN4791 is in service from Hertford garage near the end of its life. J.F. Higham

A later version of the Invader was known as the Centaur of which this example was bought by Martin & King (Nippy Bus Service) of Windsor in 1932. The provenance of the body of JB568 is unknown but the roof profile is unusual and distinctive.
The Omnibus Society/J.F. Higham

The four Crossleys acquired from Filkins and Ainsworth of Harefield were the oldest buses to join the LPTB fleet. Their 25hp chassis had been built as staff cars for the Royal Flying Corps in the First World War and rebodied as buses in the early 1920s. ME6966 was a two-door twelve-seater with a Strachan body dating from 1923 and, in common with its stablemates, was withdrawn by London Transport within a couple of months of acquisition. Ken Glazier collection

The small DST class included one single-decker, this Duple-bodied CH6 coach which was acquired from West London Coaches. DST 6 was absorbed into the Private Hire fleet and remained in use until 1937 soon after this photograph was taken in Old Palace Yard outside the Houses of Parliament. The CH6 had the CV35 6-cylinder sleeve-valve 5.76 85 bhp petrol engine and, uniquely among the single-deck acquisitions, Daimler/Wilson preselective gearbox and fluid flywheel. D.W.K. Jones

A.E. Blane's Imperial Bus Service of Romford contributed a selection of Dennis single-deckers to the LPTB, including this 14-seat Metcalfe-bodied 30cwt which became DM 7 in the Central Bus fleet. These popular little 11ft wheelbase buses had 4-cylinder 2.7 litre petrol engines which developed 36bhp at 2,000 rpm. The photograph shows DM 7 operating from the remote Barking garage on the former Imperial route to Birch Road. J.F. Higham

Four 2½ ton Dennises joined the Central Bus fleet, survivors of a fleet taken over from the London Public Omnibus Company by the LGOC in 1929. They were retained in service for use on route 204, which was deemed to be unsuitable for larger vehicles, until they could be replaced by Leyland Cubs in 1936. This rear view of Dodson-bodied DS 35 at Enfield garage shows the precarious and steep steps which were encountered on single-deckers of the period. D.W.K. Jones

This later version of the 2½ ton Dennis had a Strachan body and was bought by Amersham & District in 1926. It is parked at the former Amersham & District premises after acquisition by the LPTB bearing Country Bus colours but as yet lacking a fleet name. D.W.K. Jones

The Dennis F was a normal control version of the E and had a White & Poppe 4-cylinder 6.24 litre engine which developed 70bhp at 1700rpm. This bus version of the F was inherited from LGCS who had acquired it from C. Aston of Watford in May 1933. The builder of the attractively workmanlike body is not known. J.F. Higham

The Dennis G was a bus version of the 30cwt lorry chassis and had the same 4-cylinder side-valve 2.7 litre petrol engine rated at 36bhp. KP3796, an 18-seater dating from 1929, was formerly a Gravesend & District bus but spent its last days with London Transport working in the Addlestone area. J.F. Higham

The only Dennis G in the Central Bus fleet was DM 5, a Metcalfe-bodied 18-seater taken over from A.E. Blane of Romford. It continued in service on its home territory until the arrival of the Leyland Cubs in 1936. D.W.K. Jones

A slightly longer version of the G, classified GL, was introduced in 1929 and had an overhead-valve version of the 2.72 litre engine, which developed 42bhp. KX5923 was bought in 1930 by Amersham & District who chose their favourite bodybuilder, Strachan, to supply this handsome 18-seat body. D.W.K. Jones

Twelve Dennis Lancets entered the London Transport fleet between 1933 and 1939, nine of which received numbers in the DT class. From 1931 onwards the Lancet displaced the Arrow as the single-deck equivalent of the Lance, having a similar specification except that it was powered by a smaller 85bhp 5.7 litre petrol engine. Oil engined versions were not available until 1934. Various types of Dennis figured large in the Amersham & District fleet, as did Strachan bodywork, and both came together on this 32-seat Lancet. During its LPTB years DT 3B forsook Buckinghamshire for Hertfordshire and the new Two Waters garage and was photographed in the then quiet country town of Hemel Hempstead working on route 337. The Omnibus Society

A possible successor to the Dart in London might have been the Dennis Ace had Leyland not got in first with the Cub, although an oil engine was not offered as standard at first, the usual unit being a 3.77litre 4-cylinder 60bhp petrol engine. The set-back front axle gave it this distinctive look which earned it the affectionate nickname 'flying pig'. AKR937 (later DC 1B) was one of two Waveney-bodied examples ordered by Gravesend and District but delivered directly to London Transport in 1934. Ken Glazier collection

DC 3B was a Dennis Mace, the forward control variant of the Ace, and it came to London Transport with the Penn Bus Company's fleet when it was bought in 1935. The 26-seat centre entrance body, also by Dennis, had rather small saloon windows and this unusual full-depth driver's cab door reaching down to the skirt. It was allocated to High Wycombe garage and ran until 1938. D.W.K. Jones

Another internationally famous name that could be found on London Transport's acquired small buses was Dodge, of which there were seven. HC9385 was a 20-seat Strachan-bodied GB which dated from 1928 and had belonged to Martin & King (Nippy Bus Service) of Windsor, where it was still operating when photographed during its eight month stay with the Board in 1934. J.F. Higham

When Ford Motors moved production to Dagenham, the famous model T was replaced for the home market by the AA, of which fifteen, including one six-wheeler, were absorbed by London Transport. Typical of these was KX5836, a fourteen seater which had operated with W. Thomson's T.T. Bus service of Slough, seen here at Windsor Castle sharing the stand with another 'minor types' acquisition, MY 1. J.F. Higham

Guy offered the OND and ONDF models between 1929 and 1931 as 20-seat one-man buses, both powered by Meadows 4-cylinder 3.3 litre petrol engines. The small Loumax concern bought two of the ONDF forward control type which were numbered into the G series when the LGOC acquired them. Unusually for London their bodywork was built in Lowestoft by United, forerunner of the Eastern Coach Works company. They were withdrawn by London Transport almost immediately but remained in stock for two years. This is G 8 awaiting its fate, which was to go to Thomas and James in Port Talbot. *The Omnibus Society/J.F. Higham*

Martin & King of Windsor (Nippy Bus Service) operated this Duple-bodied OND, the normal control version, which they bought third-hand in 1932 from Thames Valley who had acquired it in 1931 from the GWR. UV9121 operated for London Transport, still at Windsor, for only eight months but it was nevertheless repainted into Country Bus livery and even had the name 'GENERAL' added to the display glass above the rather cramped destination blind. *J.F. Higham*

The first models produced by Guy Motors specifically designed as buses were the BA series, introduced in 1924, a 13ft 4ins wheelbase chassis powered by a 4-cylinder 4.5 litre petrol engine. The LGOC bought six in 1928 for operation by National and these continued in service with Country Buses until 1935. UC2272, still at work in Watford, carries a conductor, who can be seen through the saloon windows about to issue tickets to two ladies in cloche hats. His presence was necessary on these small buses because they had rear entrances. J.F. Higham

Among the vehicles acquired by LGCS when the Great Western Railway services at Slough were taken over in 1932, were four Guy FBBs all dating from 1927. Two were coaches, which were numbered G 1 and 2 in the Green Line series, and two buses which were never numbered. The buses had 32-seat Hall Lewis bodywork as illustrated here on YH6819 when it was awaiting disposal and its eventual fate as a showman's bus. The FBB was Guy Motors' first forward control bus model, launched in 1926, and had the same mechanical specification as the BA type. H.J. Snook/Ken Glazier collection

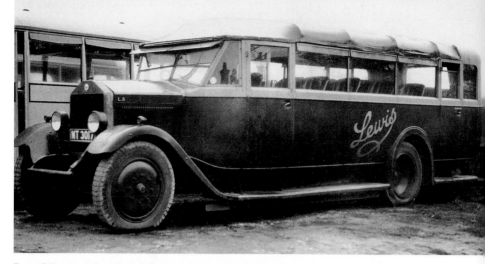

Four of the seven Lancias briefly owned by London Transport came from the Lewis Omnibus Company of Watford, all Pentaiotas. These were powered by a Lancia 60bhp petrol engine with transmission through a four-speed crash gearbox. MT3017 had been a Lancia demonstrator when it was new in 1929 with this 26-seat 'all weather' coach body of unknown provenance but its relative youth did not rescue it from the drive for standardisation and it was removed from the fleet in October 1934. It saw another nine years service with Boddy & Son of Bridlington. Ken Glazier collection

The PLSC3 was the long wheelbase version of the Leyland Lion (16ft 5ins) suitable for 26ft-long bodywork, the maximum allowed in London when it was built in 1928, and powered by a 5.1 litre petrol engine. LN 2, formerly owned by Peraeque of Stockwell who had run it on route 50 (Streatham–Lonesome), was allocated to Old Kent Road for route 202. The position of the conductor inside the open rear entrance shows how little space there was for him to stand and keep the platform clear. Ken Glazier collection

The new style of radiator on Birch-bodied LN 7 is the clue that this is a Lion LT1, the successor to the PLSC3, which had a wheelbase of 16ft 7¼ins and an improved version of the 5.1 litre petrol engine. Nil Desperandum was the fleet name of R.Hawkins of Rotherhithe, another operator on the 202, and his buses joined the others at Old Kent Road, where they all remained until the 5Q5s arrived in 1936. D.W.K. Jones

The normal control equivalent of the LT1 was the Lioness LTB1, which had the same 6-cylinder 6.8 litre 98 bhp petrol engine as the Tiger. London Transport owned one, VX4069, acquired from Harris of Grays. During its two-year stay it operated on the other side of the river, from Northfleet garage. After leaving London Transport it went to Gem Coaches of Weymouth and later to Belle Coaches of Lowestoft. D.W.K. Jones

At the end of the 1920s Willys-Overland-Crossley sold chassis for 14-seat buses under the name Manchester, six of which were acquired by London Transport from Gravesend & District. The company also assembled American Willys-Overlands, hence its name, and the Manchester was therefore heavily influenced by American design practice. VX8540, a 20-seat all-weather coach, was originally owned by A.R. Greenslade (Tilbury Dock Coaches) but passed to Gravesend & District in July 1933. It was photographed in Gravesend shortly before the route changes of 16th May 1934 which signalled its withdrawal. After it was sold it became a lorry. J.F. Higham

When the Great Western Railway services in Slough were taken over by London General Country Services in 1932, five Maudslays came with them, including YW3350 which had a Buckingham 32-seat rear entrance bus body. It was an ML3 with a four-cylinder 4.94 litre overhead camshaft engine and a wheelbase of 16ft 6ins. Although it remained in stock until April 1936, it had not been embraced by Chiswick and it was never numbered. J.F. Higham

KR6859 was a Manchester LWV 2-ton 19-seat bus built in 1930 and owned by Gravesend & District. It does not look long for this world in this photograph and did little work as a bus for the LPTB, but it was used as a petrol lorry from July to December 1934 after which it was converted back to a bus and remained in service until 1936 (a fate similarly visited on KR7090). D.W.K. Jones

Each of the four buses acquired from Martin & King's Nippy Bus service of Windsor was different, the smallest of the quartet being this Morris Z6, a 14-seater dating from 1928 when it was owned by W.F. Clatworthy. It was photographed outside the Old Crown Hotel, Slough, during the period when Windsor garage had the code WC, which on mature reflection, the Board decided would be less offensive if restyled WR! D.W.K. Jones

Windsor (and Slough) appear frequently as background to photographs in this section because of the exceptionally large number of Independent services acquired by the Board. This Reall-bodied Morris Commercial Director, a 20-seater, came from E.A. Shand's Cream Service of Slough, whose three buses were all Morrises. The Omnibus Society/J.F. Higham

This 14-seat Morris R was another of the acquisitions from the Great Western Railway and is seen at work in Watford. The Omnibus Society/J.F. Higham

The East Surrey Traction Company had nine Morris Viceroy YB6, including Holbrook-bodied MS 2B which had been a demonstrator hence its 'foreign' registration. It remained in use until 1938, long enough for it to be attired in the new two-tone Country Bus green livery. D.W.K. Jones

Two of East Surrey's Morris Viceroys were Harrington-bodied 20-seat coaches which became part of the London Transport Private Hire fleet, remaining there until being withdrawn in 1938. The centre section of their roofs could be slid open behind the brace bar which can be seen projecting above the roof of MS 11c, just behind the door. J.F. Higham

This sorry looking beast, a product of the American Reo company, was once a proud part of the St Albans & District fleet but it met with Chiswick's disapproval and was quickly withdrawn and sold. It was a Pullman, a top-of-the-range model with a 6-cylinder 50bhp engine and three-speed gearbox. It was new in 1926 when it had been bought by South Coast Coaches of Folkestone but it was never heard of again once it left London Transport. D.W.K. Jones

Adding further piquancy to the international flavour brought to the LPTB fleet by these small operators, this 40hp Swiss-built Saurer had a Duple body and had been one of two operated by West London Coaches on their Aylesbury and Chesham express services. Still at work on the Aylesbury route, XY5357 now wears the Green Line emblem. The Omnibus Society/J.F. Higham

Star produced bus chassis for only eleven years and although they had a reputation for being well made they were hand-made and expensive which no doubt contributed to their downfall. The Star Flyer, first appeared in 1927 and had a six-cylinder 3.2 litre 60bhp engine with a claimed top speed of 50mph. JB292 was a late example, bought in 1932 by Moore (Imperial Bus Service) of Windsor, who handed it over to the Board with their Windsor Hospital–Langley service. The star on the top of the radiator filler cap was a symbol repeated on several parts of the chassis. H.J. Snook/ Ken Glazier collection

Nine Thurgood-bodied 20-seat Thornycrofts were taken from the fleet of Peoples Motor Services of Ware and remained in service long enough to be numbered NY 1–9. NY 6B remained in stock until 1938 when the small buses on local routes in the Addlestone area were replaced by large saloons. It then found a new home with C. Collier of Abertillery. D.W.K. Jones

The interior of one of the small Thornycrofts, showing the overlay of Chiswick influence in London Transport ownership, notably in the seat moquette and the uncovered light bulbs. D.W.K. Jones

Three Thornycroft BCs with 22-seat Vickers coach bodies were included in the deal when the Great Western Railway sold its Slough interests to LGCS in 1932. They were allocated to Green Line Coaches Ltd and were given the numbers TH 1–3 but they did not survive long with London Transport. The BC, sometimes known as the Boadicea, had a 33.8hp 6-cylinder engine and was reputed to have an enviable performance, being capable of speeds up to 60mph and of fast hill climbing. D.W.K. Jones

The Thornycroft Cygnet was introduced in 1932 and Peoples Motor Services of Ware bought three the same year, all bodied by the local firm Thurgood. JH 3432 was a forward control example and is seen at Windsor showing all too clearly that an attempt to give its radiator a more modern appearance has failed signally. Ken Glazier collection

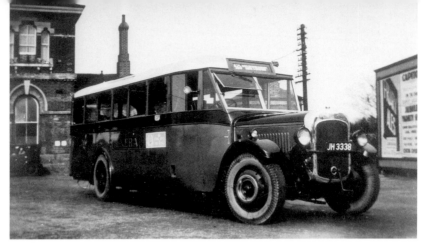

Also from Peoples of Ware JH3338, seen here at Dorking North station, was a normal control control Cygnet. Ken Glazier collection

The smart and neat body of PG2018, a 1929-built Thornycroft A2L, was supplied by the Nottingham firm of Challands Ross who were apparently favoured by its original owners Woking & District. It was one of the buses which moved to East Surrey as part of an agreement to purchase the company jointly with Aldershot & District.
Ken Glazier collection

Apart from the petrol-electrics in the 'O' class, the LPTB also became the owner of eleven conventional petrol-engined Tilling Stevens vehicles from the Express B9 and B10 model ranges, one of which was a double-decker. All had 4-cylinder 40hp petrol engines. Maidstone & District was the origin of six of these, including Short Bros-bodied B9A KM3866. In its short time with the London Transport it abandoned Kent in favour of Buckinghamshire and is seen at Chesham on the local route to Bellingdon.
J.F. Higham

MINOR TYPES (Number acquired shown in brackets)

Identity	Chassis model	Body make	Seats	Acquired from	New	Date Into stock	Date out of stock
AJS (5)							
PG9385	Pilot	Petty	B26F	LGCS (formerly Woking & District)	1930	1.7.33	10.34
KX7469	Pilot	Petty	B20F	Amersham & District Motor Bus and Haulage Co. Ltd	1931	24.11.33	10.34
* VX4253	Pilot	Metcalfe	B25F	A.E. Blane (Imperial Bus Service), Romford	1930	28.11.34	9.7.35
UR7002	Pilot	Petty	B24F	Elite, Watford	1930	30.8.33	9.34
UR8528	Pilot	Petty	B24F	Elite, Watford	1931	30.8.33	9.34
* Numbered AJS 1							
ALBION (10)							
* YU2972	Viking PK26	Vickers	B26F	Lewis Omnibus Co., Watford	1927	1.10.33	16.4.36
YU2973	Viking PK26	"	B26F	Lewis Omnibus Co., Watford	1927	1.10.33	25.4.36
YU2974	Viking PK26	"	B26F	Lewis Omnibus Co., Watford	1927	1.10.33	23.4.36
YU2975	Viking PK26	"	B26F	Lewis Omnibus Co., Watford	1927	1.10.33	10.34
UV5761	Viking PKB26	Not known	C28F	Lewis Omnibus Co., Watford	1929	1.10.33	23.4.36
CH7935	Viking PM28	LMS Rly	B32R	LGCS (formerly London Midland & Scottish Rly)	1929	1.7.33	14.4.36
UR3580	Viking PM28	London Lorries	B32R	LGCS (formerly Prentice; Chiltern Bus, Tring)	1929	1.7.33	7.5.36
R06648	Viking PN26	Not known	B26?	LGCS (formerly Prentice; Chiltern Bus, Tring)	1927	1.7.33	2.34
UR228	Viking PNA26	Not known	C26?	LGCS (formerly Prentice; Chiltern Bus, Tring)	1928	1.7.33	10.34
AHK984	Valkyrie PV70	Duple	FC31F	Sunset Pullman Coaches Ltd	1933	25.1.34	11.3.38
* Numbered AN1C							
BAT (1)							
UR8310	3X	Not known	B20C	St Albans & District (Charles Russett & Son)	1930	10.11.33	10.34
BEAN (12)							
* MV933	WC	Birch	B14F	LGOC (formerly Royal Highlander)	1931	1.7.33	29.7.36
* HX3466	W	Birch	B14F	LGOC (formerly Royal Highlander)	1931	1.7.33	20.12.34
* HX3467	W	Birch	B14F	LGOC (formerly Royal Highlander)	1931	1.7.33	29.7.36
* MY3496	W	Willowbrook	B18F	LGOC (formerly Pinner Bus)	1930	1.7.33 c	29.7.35
* DV5364	H	Tiverton Coachworks	B20F	H. F. Phillips, Hornchurch	1930	15.12.33	26.7.35
EV2060	W	Strachan	B18F	Stephens' Rainham Bus Services (A.A.W. Stephens)			
GJ5077	W	Willowbrook	B14F	London General Country Services Ltd	1930	1.7.33	25.9.34
KX4018	HW	Not known	B20F	F. Berry, Slough	1930	15.3.34	25.9.34
RF5806	W	Willowbrook	B20F	London General Country Services Ltd	1929	1.7.33	9.34
RX7554	HW	Duple	B14F	F.C. Owens, Slough	1930	2.2.34	10.34
UR6278	W	Thurgood	B14F	St. Albans & District (Charles Russett & Son)	1930	10.11.33	26.10.34
UR6279	W	Birch	B20R	St. Albans & District (Charles Russett & Son)	1930	10.11.33	26.10.34
* Numbered BN 1–5							
BRISTOL (4)							
R07064	B	Strachan	C32F	Lewis Omnibus Co., Watford	1927	1.10.33	10.34
R07065	B	Strachan	C32F	Lewis Omnibus Co., Watford	1927	1.10.33	10.34
UR3831	B	Strachan	B32R	Lewis Omnibus Co., Watford	1929	1.10.33	15.5.36
UR3832	B	Strachan	B32R	Lewis Omnibus Co., Watford	1929	1.10.33	7.5.36
BROCKWAY (1)							
WU6266		Not known	B20?	Ben Stanley, Hersham	1926	24.4.34	25.9.34
CHEVROLET (33)							
* TW8532	LM	Metcalfe	B14F	C & A Roberts & E. Hammer (Romford & District)	1927	11.7.34	26.7.35
* YU9022	LM	Metcalfe	B14F	A.E. Blane (Imperial Bus Service), Romford	1927	28.11.34	27.7.35
GC5531	LQ	Not known	B14F	Barton & Johnson (Elite Omnibus Co), Watford	1930	30.8.33	25.9.34
GK9584	U	Not known	B14F	F.W. Bell, Slough (Bell's Bus Service)	1930	10.5.34	10.34
GJ3757	U	Willowbrook	C14F	F.W. Bell, Slough (Bell's Bus Service)	1930	10.5.34	5.34
G09046	U	Thurgood	B14F	Amersham & District Motor Bus and Haulage Co. Ltd	1931	24.11.33	10.34
HX9676	U	Reall	B14F	F.W. Bell, Slough (Bell's Bus Service)	1930	10.5.34	10.34
HX9677	U	Reall	B14F	F. Berry, Slough	1930	15.3.34	10.34
KX1343	LP	Hoyal	B14F	A.H. Lucas, Slough	1928	26.4.34	25.9.34

KX1580	LP	Willmott	B14F	Amersham & District Motor Bus and Haulage Co. Ltd	1928	24.11.33	4.34
KX3075	LQ	Not known	B14F	F.W. Bell, Slough (Bell's Bus Service)	1929	10.5.34	5.35
KX4076	LQ	Not known	B14F	W. Thomson (TT Bus Service), Slough	1930	8.2.34	5.35
KX4530	LQ	Not known	B14F	W. Thomson (TT Bus Service), Slough	1930	8.2.34	5.35
KX4534	LQ	Not known	B14F	R.J. Last (Speedwell Bus Service), Windsor	1930	3.5.34	5.35
KX5977	U	Not known	B14F	F.S. Bowler, Beaconsfield	1930	28.4.34	10.34
KX6513	U	Not known	B14F	Amersham & District Motor Bus and Haulage Co. Ltd	1931	24.11.33	10.34
KX7490	U	Willmott	B14F	A.H. Lucas, Slough	1931	26.4.34	9.34
MY9839	LQ	Not known	B14F	F.W. Edwards (Edwards' Motor Services), Rainham	1930	6.1.34	9.34
PG7703	LQ	Not known	B14F	A.R. Rudall (The Magnet Omnibus Service), Guildford	1930	8.3.34	10.34
PG9110	LQ	Not known	B14F	Drake & Lucas (The Egham Motor Company)	1930	17.2.34	25.9.34
PH6509	LM	Not known	B14F	A.R. Rudall (The Magnet Omnibus Service), Guildford	1928	8.3.34	10.34
PK6935	LQ	Not known	B14F	R.G. Harwood, Weybridge	1929	17.1.34	25.9.34
PL1211	U	Not known	B14F	J.W. Didcock (The Reo Omnibus Co.), Addlestone	1930	19.12.33	25.9.34
RO8517	LM	Thurgood	B14F	Peoples Motor Services Ltd, Ware	1927	1.12.33	10.34
RX7617	U	Not known	B14F	R.J. Last (Speedwell Bus Service), Windsor	1930	3.5.34	9.34
RX7545	U	Hoyal	B14F	A.H. Lucas, Slough	1930	26.9.34	9.34
UC6438	LM	Not known	B14F	S.H. Viles (The Pioneer Omnibus Co.), Apsley End	1928	27.1.34	5.35
UR3273	LQ	Not known	B14F	LGCS (formerly A.E. Gilbert, Essendon)	1929	1.7.33	5.35
UR4218	LQ	Not known	B14F	H.G.Biggerstaff, Sarratt	1929	10.5.34	5.35
UV9957	LQ	Not known	B16F	W.M. Short (Y.S. Coaches), Watford	1929	30.8.33	25.9.34
UW7614	LQ	Not known	B14F	R.H. Clark (Clark's Motor Coaches)	1929	18.5.34	10.34
UW6727	LQ	Not known	B14F	F.W. Bell, Slough (Bell's Bus Service)	1929	10.5.34	10.34
VX4074	LQ	Furber	B14F	City Coach Co. Ltd (formerly Regent, Brentwood)	1930	21.8.36	16.6.37

* These two were numbered CH 4 and 5

COMMER (13)

GN4790	Invader	Weymann	C18F	London General Country Services Ltd	1931	1.7.33	23.4.36
GN4791	Invader	Weymann	C18F	London General Country Services Ltd	1931	1.7.33	16.4.36
GN4792	Invader	Weymann	C18F	London General Country Services Ltd	1931	1.7.33	7.4.36
GN4793	Invader	Weymann	C18F	London General Country Services Ltd	1931	1.7.33	23.4.36
GN4794	Invader	Weymann	C18F	London General Country Services Ltd	1931	1.7.33	23.4.36
GN4795	Invader	Weymann	C18F	London General Country Services Ltd	1931	1.7.33	23.4.36
G09129	6TK	Not known	B20F	F.R. Harris (Harris's Coaches), Grays	1931	18.5.34	23.4.36
GP9279	6TK	Not known	B20F	Smith & Godden (The Reliable Omnibus & Motor Coaches)	1931	31.5.34	8.5.36
GP9555	6TK	Not known	B20F	Smith & Godden (The Reliable Omnibus & Motor Coaches)	1931	31.5.34	8.5.36
HW6290	N4	Not known	B20?	Charles Russett & Son (St Albans & District)	1929	10.11.33	10.35
JB568	T20X	Not known	B20F	Martin & King (Nippy Bus Service) Windsor	1932	7.2.34	23.4.36
UR6671	6TK	Strachan	B20F	F.J. Cobb (Albanian Bus Co)	1930	17.2.34	8.35
UR9874	6TK	Strachan	B20F	F.J. Cobb (Albanian Bus Co)	1931	17.2.34	8.5.36

CROSSLEY (4)

ME6966		Strachan	B12D	Filkins & Ainsworth, Harefield	1923	1.11.33	10.34
MH1852		Strachan	B14F	Filkins & Ainsworth, Harefield	1924	1.11.33	10.34
MY1959		Strachan	B12D	Filkins & Ainsworth, Harefield	1924	1.11.33	10.34
OE5780		Strachan	B14F	Filkins & Ainsworth, Harefield	1921	1.11.33	10.34

DAIMLER (4)

GU2736	CMR	Strachan	C26?	A.A.W. Stephens (Stephens' Rainham Omnibus Service)	1929	16.3.34	10.34
PE6984	CM36	Not known	B26D	LGCS (formerly Woking & District)	1925	1.7.33	3.34
PE8642	CM36	Not known	B26?	LGCS (formerly Woking & District)	1925	1.7.33	3.34
UR4642	CF6	Bamber	C26F	Flower & Etches (City Omnibus Service), St Albans	1929	29.3.34	10.34

DENNIS (Does not include DA, DE or DL classes which will be found in separate listings) (69)

As such a large number of Dennis single-deckers were acquired by the LPTB, these are listed by model to aid clarity.

n7 VA4584	30cwt	Strachan	B18F	C & A Roberts & E. Hammer (Romford & District Motor Services)	1925	10.7.34	27.7.35
n7 EV4010	30cwt	Metcalfe	B14F	C & A Roberts & E. Hammer (Romford & District Motor Services)	1931	10.7.34	22.6.35
n5 VX6739	30cwt	Thurgood	B14F	A.E. Blane Ltd (Imperial Bus Service), Romford	1930	28.11.34	12.7.35
n5 VX7401	30cwt	Metcalfe	B14F	A.E. Blane Ltd (Imperial Bus Service), Romford	1930	28.11.34	2.9.36
n5 VX7354	30cwt	Thurgood	B14F	A.E. Blane Ltd (Imperial Bus Service), Romford	1930	28.11.34	12.7.35

Reg	Class	Chassis/Body	Body	Operator	Year	Date 1	Date 2
DY4622	30cwt	Not known	C18?	Gravesend & District Bus Services Ltd	1927	1.10.33	10.34
GC1313	30cwt	Wilmott	B14F	Smith & Godden (The Reliable Omnibus & Motor Coaches)	1930	31.5.34	10.34
GU7544	30cwt	Not known	B14F	A. Howes (Howes's Brown Bus), Englefield Green	1929	23.3.34	11.35
n9 KO6244	30cwt	Vickers	B14F	West Kent Motor Services Ltd	1927	3.10.39	†
KP59	30cwt	Not known	B18F	Gravesend & District Bus Services Ltd	1928	1.10.33	18.4.36
KP1587	30cwt	Not known	B18F	Gravesend & District Bus Services Ltd	1928	1.10.33	25.4.36
n9 KR5018	30cwt	Short Bros	B14F	F.W. Edwards (Edwards' Motor Services)	1930	3.10.39	†
PG3194	30cwt	Not known	B18F	W. Eggleton Ltd, Woking	1930	2.6.34	23.4.36
PG8716	30cwt	Not known	B18F	W. Eggleton Ltd, Woking	1930	2.6.34	25.4.36
PH5276	30cwt	Not known	B18F	W. Eggleton Ltd, Woking	1927	2.6.34	16.4.36
PP7700	30cwt	Strachan	B14F	Amersham & District Motor Bus and Haulage Co. Ltd	1927	24.11.33	10.34
n4 MH8183	2½ ton	Dodson	B25R	London General Omnibus Co. (formerly London Public O.Co.)	1925	1.7.33	16.6.37
n4 YL966	2½ ton	Dodson	B26R	London General Omnibus Co. (formerly London Public O.Co.)	1925	1.7.33	29.7.36
n4 RO1596	2½ ton	Strachan &	B26R	London General Omnibus Co. Brown (formerly London Public O.Co.)	1925	1.7.33	29.7.36
n4 NK8877	2½ ton	Dodson	B20R	London General Omnibus Co. (formerly London Public O.Co.)	1924	1.7.33	29.7.36
PP2245	2½ ton	Wycombe (1928 body)	B20R	The Penn Bus Co. Ltd.	c 1924	1.8.35	24.8.36
PP4089	2½ ton	Strachan	B28?	Amersham & District Motor Bus and Haulage Co. Ltd	1925	24.11.33	10.4.36
PP5254	2½ ton	Strachan	B26F	Amersham & District Motor Bus and Haulage Co. Ltd	1926	24.11.33	10.34
PP5454	2½ ton	Strachan	B26F	Amersham & District Motor Bus and Haulage Co. Ltd	1926	24.11.33	10.34
PP7144	2½ ton	Strachan	B28?	Amersham & District Motor Bus and Haulage Co. Ltd	1926	24.11.33	23.4.36
PP7251	2½ ton	Strachan	B26R	Amersham & District Motor Bus and Haulage Co. Ltd	1926	24.11.33	7.5.36
PH1106	4 ton	Strachan	B25R	LGCS (formerly Aldershot & District Traction Co.)	1927	1.7.33	10.4.36
PP3477	4 ton	Strachan	B31R	Amersham & District Motor Bus and Haulage Co. Ltd	1925	24.11.33	10.34
KX470	F	Strachan	C30R	Amersham & District Motor Bus and Haulage Co. Ltd	1928	24.11.33	10.34
RO9211	F	Not known	B26?	LGCS (formerly C. Aston, Watford)	1928	1.7.33	6.5.36
RO9807	F	Not known	B26?	LGCS (formerly C. Aston, Watford)	1928	1.7.33	10.4.36
GP5047	GL	Not known	B20F	Smith & Godden (The Reliable Omnibus & Motor Coaches)	1931	31.5.34	23.4.36
KO7272	G	Vickers	B14F	West Kent Motor Services Ltd	1928	‡4.10.39	‡‡
KP3796	G	Not known	B18F	Gravesend & District Bus Services Ltd	1929	1.10.33	5.35
KP4951	G	Not known	B18F	Gravesend & District Bus Services Ltd	1929	1.10.33	10.35
KP7159	G	Not known	B18F	Gravesend & District Bus Services Ltd	1929	1.10.33	5.35
KR348	G	Red & White	B18F	Gravesend & District Bus Services Ltd	1929	1.10.33	10.35
KR705	G	Not known	B18F	Gravesend & District Bus Services Ltd	1929	1.10.33	15.1.36
KX1326	G	Strachan	B18F	Amersham & District Motor Bus and Haulage Co. Ltd	1928	24.11.33	28.4.36
OT8598	G	Strachan	B18F	Aldershot & District Traction Co. Ltd	1928	2.8.33	18.5.36
VW6182	G	Not known	C20F	Smith & Godden (The Reliable Omnibus & Motor Coaches)	1928	31.5.34	1934
VW7400	G	Not known	B14F	Smith & Godden (The Reliable Omnibus & Motor Coaches)	1928	31.5.34	6.34
n6 VX3180	G	Metcalfe	B18F	A.E. Blane (Imperial Bus Service), Romford	1928	28.11.34	23.7.36
XV6303	G	Not known	B14F	A. Howes (Howes's Brown Bus), Englefield Green	1929	23.3.34	11.35
KX5923	GL	Strachan	B18F	Amersham & District Motor Bus and Haulage Co. Ltd	1930	24.11.33	6.5.36
n8 GJ2307	GL	Duple	B20F	C & A Roberts & E. Hammer (Romford & District Motor Services)	1930	11.7.34	2.9.36
n8 VX9897	GL	Duple	B18F	C & A Roberts & E. Hammer (Romford & District Motor Services)	1931	11.7.34	4.8.36
KX5967	GL	Strachan	B18F	Amersham & District Motor Bus and Haulage Co. Ltd	1930	24.11.33	8.4.36
KX8569	GL	Strachan	B18F	Amersham & District Motor Bus and Haulage Co. Ltd	1932	24.11.33	28.4.36
PL5896	GL	Not known	B20F	W. Eggleton Ltd, Woking	1931	2.6.34	25.4.36
VX6341	GL	Thurgood	B20?	F.W. Edwards (Edwards' Motor Services)	1930	6.1.34	23.4.36
n1 AKR937	Ace	Waveney	B20F	Ordered by Gravesend & District Bus Services Ltd	1934	25.3.34	11.7.38

n1 BPF318	Ace	Waveney	B20F	Ordered by Gravesend & District Bus Services			
					1934	27.3.34	18.7.38
CKL719	Ace	Dennis	B20F	West Kent Motor Services Ltd	1936	‡ 4.10.39	**
DPD859	Ace	Dennis	B20R	A.T. Locke (Blue Saloon Coaches) via			
				Aldershot & District	1935	‡ 12.1.38	29.3.38
EPK29	Ace	Dennis	B20R	A.T. Locke (Blue Saloon Coaches) via			
				Aldershot & District	1937	‡ 12.1.38	29.3.38
n2 AKE711	Lancet	Duple	C32R	Gravesend & District Bus Services Ltd	1933	1.10.33	9.3.38
n2 JH4678	Lancet	Thurgood	B32?	G.W. Currell (White Heather Bus Service),			
				Knebworth	1933	4.5.34	5.5.38
n2 KX8570	Lancet	Strachan	B32R	Amersham & District Motor Bus and Haulage			
				Co. Ltd	1932	24.11.33	4.5.38
n2 JJ1836	Lancet	Duple	C32R	E. Puttergill (Golden Arrow) Stockwell	1933	24.11.33	18.3.38
n2 JJ1837	Lancet	Duple	C32R	E. Puttergill (Golden Arrow) Stockwell	1933	24.11.33	11.3.38
n2 EV4760	Lancet	Metcalf	B32F	A.E. Blane (Imperial Bus Service), Romford	1932	28.11.34	4.5.38
n2 EV6168	Lancet	Metcalf	B32F	A.E. Blane (Imperial Bus Service), Romford	1932	28.11.34	6.5.38
n2 ABH350	Lancet	Dennis	B32?	The Penn Bus Co. Ltd	1933	1.8.35	5.5.38
n2 BKX696	Lancet	Dennis	B32C	The Penn Bus Co. Ltd	1933	1.8.35	16.3.38
AJH870	Lancet	Thurgood	B32F	H. Aston (Berkhamsted & District Motor			
				Services)	1935	‡ 1.3.39	11.4.39
BRO247	Lancet	Duple	B32F	H. Aston (Berkhamsted & District Motor			
				Services)	1936	‡ 1.3.39	11.4.39
EPL628	Lancet	Dennis	C32F	A.T. Locke (Blue Saloon Coaches) via			
				Aldershot & District	1937	‡ 12.1.38	29.3.38
n3 BBH755	Mace	Dennis	B26C	The Penn Bus Co. Ltd	1934	1.8.35	5.9.38

n D 2 in the Green Line numbering scheme   n1 Numbered DC 1B, 2B
n2 Numbered DT 1c, 2c, 3B, 4c–7c, 8B, 9B; DT 4–6 were at first allocated to Central Buses and given the numbers
    DL 29, 30, 35, 34 respectively; renumbered in DT series when transferred to Country Buses on 17.1.34 (DT 4, 5) or
    12.2.35 (DT 6, 7)
n3 Numbered DC 3B   n4 Numbered DS 7, 15, 34, 35 respectively
n5 Numbered DM 6–8 respectively   n6 Numbered DM 5
n7 Numbered DM 1 and 2   n8 Numbered DM 3 and 4
n9 Numbered D 202B and D 203B   ‡   Taken into stock unlicensed and never operated

†, ‡‡, ** - still in stock unlicensed on 31.12 39, sold on 3.1.40†, 4.1.40‡‡, 10.1.40**

DODGE (7)

HC9385	GB	Strachan	B20F	Martin & King (Nippy Bus Service) Windsor	1928	7.2.34	10.34
KX6059	DVP	Waveney	B14F	G.H. & A.H. Lucas, Slough	1930	26.4.34	25.9.34
KX6551		Not known	B14F	F.C. Owen, Slough	1931	2.2.34	25.9.34
ML5975	A	Strachan	B20F	F. Steer (Colne Coaches)	1927	1.11.33	10.34
MP2121	A	Strachan	B20?	F.J. Cobb (Albanian Bus Co)	1928	17.2.34	10.34
MP3498	TDX	Strachan	B20F	F. Steer (Colne Coaches)	1928	1.11.33	10.34
UR4246	D	Not known	B20F	E.A. Griffiths (Victoria Omnibus Service)	1929	17.3.34	10.34

FORD (18)

HM9912	AA 6-wheel	Reynolds	B20F	Day & Beddingfield, Stanford-le-Hope	1929	30.7.34	5.35
JH1025	AA	Thurgood	B20?	F. Rowe, Aston	1931	27.4.34	7.35
KR9537	AA	Not known	B20F	H.D. Fletcher (The Enterprise Motor Service)	1931	14.11.33	5.35
				Gravesend			
KX5836	AA	Not known	B14F	W. Thomson (T.T. Bus Service), Slough	1930	8.2.34	5.35
KX5998	AA	Not known	B14F	V.S. Francis (The Royal Blue Motor Bus),	1930	15.3.34	25.9.34
				Slough			
KX6321	AA	Not known	B14F	W. Thomson (T.T. Bus Service), Slough	1931	8.2.34	5.35
MV8170	AA	Not known	B20F	H.R. Clarke (Clarke's Blue Bus Service)	1932	26.4.34	5.35
				Stoke Poges			
PJ856	AA	Not known	B16F	J.W. Didcock (The Reo Omnibus Co), Addlestone	1931	19.12.33	7.34
PK9774	AA	Not known	B14F	A. Howes (Howes' Brown Bus), Englefield Green	1929	23.3.34	10.34
PK9963	AA	Not known	B14F	B.S. Stanley (Ben Stanley), Hersham	1929	24.4.34	5.35
PL5849	AA	Not known	B18R	B.S. Stanley (Ben Stanley), Hersham	1931	24.4.34	5.35
PL5906	AA	Not known	B14F	B.S. Stanley (Ben Stanley), Hersham	1931	24.4.34	10.34
UR8133	AA	Thurgood	B20F	R.C. Knowles, Little Berkhamsted	1930	1.2.34	7.35
UR9699	AA	Not known	B20?	G.W. Currell (White Heather Bus Service)	1931	4.5.34	10.34
AKE124	AA	Not known	B20?	H.M. Howells (Greenhithe & District Bus			
				Services), Dartford	1932	18.4.34	15.1.36
ANO33	V8	Willett	B20?	J. Kirby (Karriyu Coaches) St Albans	1933	9.11.33	5.35
ANO500	V8	Willett	B20?	J. Kirby (Karriyu Coaches) St Albans	1933	9.11.33	5.35
BKO508	V8	Willett	B20F	West Kent Motor Services Ltd	1935	† 4.10.39	2.1.40

† Taken into stock unlicensed and never operated

GMC (9)

* MT6523	T30	Not known	C20F	London General Country Services Ltd	1929	1.7.33	21.5.36
* MT7818	T30	Not known	B20F	London General Country Services Ltd	1929	1.7.33	23.4.36
UR44	T40	Not known	B20?	F.J. Cobb (Albanian Bus Company)	1929	17.2.34	10.34
UR2932	T30	Strachan	B20F	F.J. Cobb (Albanian Bus Company)	1929	17.2.34	10.34

UR4013	B	Not known	B20F	F.J. Cobb (Albanian Bus Company)	1929	17.2.34	10.34
UR4238	T30	Not known	B20?	Flower & Etches (City Omnibus Services) St Albans	1929	29.3.34	10.34
UR4480	B	Not known	B20F	F.J. Cobb (Albanian Bus Company)	1929	17.2.34	10.34
UR4481	B	Not known	B20F	F.J. Cobb (Albanian Bus Company)	1929	17.2.34	10.34
UR7859	T30	Strachan	B26?	A. Barnes (Reliance Coaches), St Albans	1930	6.2.34	10.34

* These two were numbered GM 1 and 2 respectively

GUY (30)

n UR9195	OND	Duple	B20F	London General Omnibus Co. (formerly Royal Highlander)	1931	1.7.33	4.8.36
n UR9900	OND	Duple	B20F	London General Omnibus Co. (formerly Royal Highlander)	1931	1.7.33	18.7.36
n UR9997	OND	Duple	B20F	London General Omnibus Co. (formerly Royal Highlander)	1931	1.7.33	30.7.36
n UR9998	OND	Duple	B20F	London General Omnibus Co. (formerly Royal Highlander)	1931	1.7.33	30.7.36
n UR9899	OND	Duple	B20F	London General Omnibus Co. (formerly Royal Highlander)	1931	1.7.33	18.7.36
n MY4117	ONDF	United	B20F	London General Omnibus Co. (formerly Loumax)	1930	1.7.33	20.6.35
n MY3390	ONDF	United	B20F	London General Omnibus Co. (formerly Loumax)	1930	1.7.33	26.7.35
n1 YF6817	FBB	Buckingham	C32FR	London General Country Services Ltd (formerly GWR)	1927	1.7.33	3.34
n2 YH1941	FBB	Buckingham	C32FR	London General Country Services Ltd (formerly GWR)	1927	1.7.33	3.34
DH5901	BB	Vickers	B30D	Charles Russett & Son (St Albans & District)	1927	10.11.33	4.34
JH983	OND	Not known	B14F	J. Kirby (Karriyu Coaches) St. Albans	1931	9.11.33	23.4.36
MP4406	FBB	Waveney	B31D	Charles Russett & Son (St Albans & District)	1928	10.11.33	10.34
MP4958	BA	Not known	C20?	W.D. Beaumont & A.W. Priest (Beaumont's Safeway Coaches	1928	28.4.34	10.34
PJ5970	Victory	United	B20F	A.T. Locke (Blue Saloon Coaches) via Aldershot & District	1932	† 12.1.38	29.3.38
RO4574	BB	Not known	B26?	London General Country Services Ltd (formerly Watford O. Co.	1926	1.7.33	3.34
RO5301	BB	Not known	B26?	London General Country Services Ltd (formerly Watford O. Co.	1926	1.7.33	3.34
UC2267	BA	Not known	B20R	London General Country Services Ltd	1928	1.7.33	5.35
UC2268	BA	Not known	B20R	London General Country Services Ltd	1928	1.7.33	5.35
UC2269	BA	Not known	B20R	London General Country Services Ltd	1928	1.7.33	5.35
UC2270	BA	Not known	B20R	London General Country Services Ltd	1928	1.7.33	5.35
UC2271	BA	Not known	B20R	London General Country Services Ltd	1928	1.7.33	5.35
UC2272	BA	Not known	B20R	London General Country Services Ltd	1928	1.7.33	5.35
UK6253	OND	Duple	B20F	London General Country Services Ltd	1928	1.7.33	9.34
UV9120	OND	Duple	B18F	London General Country Services Ltd (formerly GWR)	1929	1.7.33	9.34
UV9121	OND	Duple	B18F	R.G. Martin & F.M. King (Nippy Bus Service), Windsor	1929	7.2.34	10.34
YH1936	FBB	Vickers	B32R	London General Country Services Ltd (formerly GWR)	1927	1.7.33	10.34
YH6819	FBB	Hall Lewis	B32R	London General Country Services Ltd (formerly GWR)	1927	1.7.33	10.34
APG207	Victory	United	B20F	A.T. Locke (Blue Saloon Coaches) via Aldershot & District	1933	† 12.1.38	29.3.38
CPA875	Wolf	Beadle	B20F	A.T. Locke (Blue Saloon Coaches) via Aldershot & District	1934	† 12.1.38	29.3.38
CPE222	Wolf	Beadle	B20F	A.T. Locke (Blue Saloon Coaches) via Aldershot & District	1935	† 12.1.38	29.3.38

n These seven numbered G 1, 3–8 respectively   n2 These two numbered G 1 and 2 in the Green Line series
† Taken into stock unlicensed and never operated

INTERNATIONAL (1)

KM2539	Not known	B15?	Gravesend & District Bus Services Ltd	1926	1.10.33	3.34

KARRIER (3)

* UL4686	JKL	Abbott	B30R	G.E. Allitt & Sons Ltd, Rotherhithe	1929	5.12.33	15.7.35
* GU2533	JKL	Dodson	B30R	G.E. Allitt & Sons Ltd, Rotherhithe	1929	5.12.33	28.6.35
RO2879	Coaster	Not known	C32F	Lewis Omnibus Co., Watford	1926	1.10.33	10.34

* Numbered KR 1 and 2 respectively

LAFFLY (2)

UR1115	LCSB	Thurgood	B26F	Peoples Motor Services Ltd, Ware	1928	1.12.33	10.34
UR1473	LCSB	Thurgood	B26F	Peoples Motor Services Ltd, Ware	1928	1.12.33	10.34

LANCIA (7)

MT3017	Pentaiota	Not known	C26D	Lewis Omnibus Co., Watford	1929	1.10.33	10.34

RO4796	Pentaiota	Not known	B26D	Lewis Omnibus Co., Watford	1926	1.10.33	10.34
RO5631	Pentaiota	Strachan	C26D	Lewis Omnibus Co., Watford	1927	1.10.33	10.34
UR181	Pentaiota	Strachan	C26?	Lewis Omnibus Co., Watford	1928	1.10.33	10.34
UR2689	Tetraiota	Not known	C26?	A. Barnes (Reliance Coaches), St Albans	1929	6.2.34	10.34
UR3157	Heptaiota	Not known	B20F	A.P. & P.B. Morgan (Comfy Coaches), Harpenden	1929	6.2.34	10.34
X03028	Tetraiota	Not known	B20F	Charles Russett & Son (St Albans & District)	1923	10.11.33	4.34

LEYLAND (except C, TD and TR classes which appear under their own headings) (27)

n K05171	Lion PLSC3	Not known	C26	LGCS Ltd	1927	1.7.33	8.4.36
n GU1500	Lion PLSC3	Not known	C32R	LGCS Ltd	1929	1.7.33	14.4.36
n GU7600	Lion PLSC3	Not known	C32R	LGCS Ltd	1929	1.7.33	14.4.36
HM8661	Lion PLSC3	Dodson	B32R	Watford Omnibus Co. Ltd	1928	1.7.33	9.4.36
VW5140	Lion PLSC3	Dodson	B32R	Watford Omnibus Co. Ltd	1928	1.7.33	7.4.36
n2 MT2992	Lion PLSC3	Dodson	B32R	G.H. Allitt & Sons Ltd, Rotherhithe	1929	1.12.33	30.7.36
n2 UC4756	Lion PLSC3	Dodson	B32R	Peraeque Transport Co. Ltd, Stockwell	1928	1.12.33	24.8.36
n2 VW5500	Lion PLSC3	Dodson	B32R	R.R. Powell & L.G. Whybrow (Chadwell), Romford	1928	13.12.33	30.7.36
n3 YX7335	Lion PLSC3	Dodson	B32R	Empress Motors Ltd, Bethnal Green	1928	30.1.34	22.8.36
n3 YX9732	Lion PLSC3	Birch	B32R	R. Hawkins & Co. Ltd (Nil Desperandum), Rotherhithe	1928	12.6.34	22.8.36
n3 YX7703	Lion PLSC3	Dodson	B32R	R. Hawkins & Co. Ltd (Nil Desperandum), Rotherhithe	1928	12.6.34	22.8.36
n3 GN7512	LT2	Birch	B30R	R. Hawkins & Co. Ltd (Nil Desperandum), Rotherhithe	1931	12.6.34	22.8.36
n3 YX7619	Lion PLSC3	Dodson	B32R	Reliance Omnibus Co. Ltd, Chingford	1928	6.11.34	28.6.35
n3 YX7620	Lion PLSC3	Dodson	B32R	Reliance Omnibus Co. Ltd, Chingford	1928	6.11.34	28.6.35
n3 XV3913	Lion PLSC3	Dodson	B32R	Reliance Omnibus Co. Ltd, Chingford	1928	6.11.34	28.6.35
n3 MP1844	Lion PLSC3	Dodson	B32R	Prince Omnibus Co. Ltd, Edmonton	1928	4.12.34	28.6.35
CH7299	Lion PLSC3	Leyland	B32F	London General Country Services Ltd (formerly LM&S Rly)	1928	1.7.33	9.4.36
CH7900	Lion PLSC3	LMS (Derby)	B32F	London General Country Services Ltd (formerly LM&S Rly)	1929	1.7.33	8.4.36
CH7902	Lion PLSC3	LMS (Derby)	B32F	London General Country Services Ltd (formerly LM&S Rly)	1929	1.7.33	7.4.36
CH7904	Lion PLSC3	LMS (Derby)	B32F	London General Country Services Ltd (formerly LM&S Rly)	1929	1.7.33	7.4.36
CH7911	Lion PLSC3	LMS (Derby)	B32F	London General Country Services Ltd (formerly LM&S Rly)	1928	1.7.33	8.4.36
CH7912	Lion PLSC3	LMS (Derby)	B32F	London General Country Services Ltd (formerly LM&S Rly)	1928	1.7.33	9.4.36
CH7914	Lion PLSC3	LMS (Derby)	B32F	London General Country Services Ltd (formerly LM&S Rly)	1928	1.7.33	8.4.36
CH7935	Lion PLSC3	LMS (Derby)	B32R	London General Country Services Ltd (formerly LM&S Rly)	1929	1.7.33	4.36
UR9034	LT1	Not known	B32F	A.R. Blowers (Express Motor Service), St Albans	1931	2.1.34	7.4.36
UR8941	LT2	Duple	B32	F.J. Cobb (Albanian Bus Co), St Albans	1931	16.2.34	7.4.36
UR9658	LT2	Not known	B32	St Albans & District (Charles Russett & Son)	1931	10.11.33	7.4.36
VX4069	LTB1	Not known	B20R	F.R. Harris (Harris's Coaches), Grays	1930	17.5.34	29.4.36

n Numbered L 1–L 3 in the Green Line series
n2 Numbered LN 1–3 (originally L 94, 95, 111 but renumbered 1.34)
n3 Numbered LN 4–11

MANCHESTER (6)

KJ4016	2-ton WLV	Not known	B20F	Gravesend & District Bus Services Ltd	1931	1.10.33	10.34
KJ4191	2-ton WLV	Not known	B20F	Gravesend & District Bus Services Ltd	1931	1.10.33	10.34
KR3034	30 cwt 6-wheel	Not known	C20F	Gravesend & District Bus Services Ltd	1930	1.10.33	10.34
KR6859	2-ton WLV	Not known	B19F	Gravesend & District Bus Services Ltd	1930	1.10.33	30.4.36
KR7090	30 cwt 6-wheel	Not known	B19F	Gravesend & District Bus Services Ltd	1930	1.10.33	26.5.36
VX8540	WLV	Not known	C20F	Gravesend & District Bus Services Ltd	1930	1.10.33	10.34

MAUDSLAY (9)

n1 GU6714	ML3B	Dodson	C24D	LGCS (formerly Bucks Expresses (Watford) Ltd)	1929	1.7.33	10.34
n1 UU820	ML3B	Dodson	C24D	LGCS (formerly Bucks Expresses (Watford) Ltd)	1929	1.7.33	10.34
n1 UU821	ML3B	Dodson	C24D	LGCS (formerly Bucks Expresses (Watford) Ltd)	1929	1.7.33	10.34
n2 YV8566	ML3	Strachan	C32D	LGCS (formerly Great Western Railway)	1928	1.7.33	2.34
n2 YV1101	ML3	Strachan	C32D	LGCS (formerly Great Western Railway)	1928	1.7.33	2.34
UU4820	ML3B	Vickers	B32R	LGCS (formerly Great Western Railway)	1929	1.7.33	6.5.36
YF1030	ML4	Not known	C26?	The Essex Omnibus Co. Ltd, East Ham	1927	10.11.33	11.5.34
YW3350	ML3	Buckingham	B32R	LGCS (formerly Great Western Railway)	1928	1.7.33	23.4.36
YW3351	ML3	Buckingham	B32R	LGCS (formerly Great Western Railway)	1928	1.7.33	24.4.36

n1 Numbered M 1–3 in the Green Line series
n2 Numbered ML 2 and 4 respectively

MINERVA (1)

	Reg	Model	Builder	Body	Operator	Year	In	Out
	KO6173		Beadle	C29?	Gravesend & District Bus Services Ltd	1927	1.10.33	3.34

MORRIS Miscellaneous models (10)

	Reg	Model	Builder	Body	Operator	Year	In	Out
	KX3813	30cwt (Z)	H. Markham	B14F	Frowen & Hill Ltd (Borough Bus), Windsor	1929	23.7.35	3.9.36
	KX3814	30cwt (Z)	H. Markham	B14F	Frowen & Hill Ltd (Borough Bus), Windsor	1929	23.7.35	3.9.36
	PF1198	l-ton n.c.	Not known	B14F	H.T. Molyneux, Bletchingley	1926	2.1.34	5.35
	RX3459	Z6	Not known	B14F	R.G. Martin & F.M. King (Nippy Bus Service), Windsor	1928	7.2.34	24.4.36
	RX5252	TX	Not known	B14F	E.A. Shand (Cream Service), Slough	1929	15.3.34	23.4.36
	RX5634	TX	Not known	B14F	E.A. Shand (Cream Service), Slough	1929	15.3.34	25.9.34
	RX5736		Duple	B20F	F.C. Owen, Slough	1929	2.2.34	25.9.34
	RX9603	Director	Reall	B20F	E.A. Shand (Cream Service), Slough	1931	15.3.34	8.4.36
	UU5009	R	Buckingham	B14F	LGCS (formerly Great Western Railway)	1929	1.7.33	23.4.36
n	VX9932	Dictator	Metcalfe	B26F	A.E. Blane Ltd (Imperial Bus Service), Romford	1931	28.11.34	18.6.35

n Numbered M 50; this was the only Morris in the Central Bus fleet and was not operated

MORRIS VICEROY (11)

	Reg	Model	Builder	Body	Operator	Year	In	Out
n	AKJ812	YB6	Duple	B20F	R.E. Hollands (Grey Motor Coach Service), Longfield	1933	17.1.34	7.6.38
n	HA7041	YB6	Holbrook	B20F	London General Country Services Ltd	1930	1.7.33	7.6.38
n	JH2585	YB6	Duple	C20F	Lewis Omnibus Co. Ltd, Watford	1932	1.10.33	7.4.36
n	PL6461	YB6	Weymann	B20F	London General Country Services Ltd	1931	1.7.33	7.6.38
n	PL6462	YB6	Weymann	B20F	London General Country Services Ltd	1931	1.7.33	7.6.38
n	PL6463	YB6	Weymann	B20F	London General Country Services Ltd	1931	1.7.33	7.6.38
n	PL6464	YB6	Weymann	B20F	London General Country Services Ltd	1931	1.7.33	7.6.38
n	PL6465	YB6	Weymann	B20F	London General Country Services Ltd	1931	1.7.33	7.6.38
n	PL6466	YB6	Weymann	B20F	London General Country Services Ltd	1931	1.7.33	7.6.38
n	PL6459	YB6	Harrington	C20F	London General Country Services Ltd	1931	1.7.33	7.6.38
n	PL6460	YB6	Harrington	C20F	London General Country Services Ltd	1931	1.7.33	7.6.38

n Numbered MS 1B–9B, 10C, 11C

OVERLAND (1)

	Reg	Model	Builder	Body	Operator	Year	In	Out
	KO3306	Not known		B16?	Gravesend & District Bus Services Ltd	1927	1.10.33	3.34

REO (8)

	Reg	Model	Builder	Body	Operator	Year	In	Out
	AG6471	Gold Crown Economy		B20F	The City Coach Co. Ltd (formerly F.H. Fuller, 'Regent'), Brentwood	1931	21.8.36	16.6.37
	EW5311	Sprinter	Not known	B20?	W.M. Short (Y.S. Coaches), Watford	1927	30.8.33	3.34
	HN6087	GB	Eaton	B24F	H.G. & F.I. Biggerstaff (Biggerstaff's Bus Service), Sarratt	1928	8.11.33	10.34
	KM4943	Pulmann	Not known	B20F	St Albans & District (Charles Russett & Son)	1926	10.11.33	10.34
	PD9246		Not known	B20F	J.W. Didcock (The Reo Omnibus Co), Chertsey	1924	19.12.33	6.34
	UR6676		Not known	B20?	J.W. Didcock (The Reo Omnibus Co), Chertsey	1930	19.12.33	25.9.34
	VX2633	Gold Crown	Not known	B20F	The City Coach Co. Ltd (formerly F.H. Fuller, 'Regent', Brentwood	1929	21.8.36	16.6.37
	VX7061	Gold Crown	Not known	B20F	R.H. Clark (Clark's Motor Coaches), West Thurrock	1930	18.5.34	4.35

SAURER (3)

	Reg	Model	Builder	Body	Operator	Year	In	Out
	RO9798	3BH	Not known	B26F	A.P. & P.B. Morgan (Comfy Coaches), Harpenden	1928	6.2.34	10.34
	XY5337	2AD	Duple	C20F	C.E. Holmes (West London Coaches), Maida Hill	1925	17.1.34	5.35
	YO5572	2BH	Birch	C14?	C.E. Holmes (West London Coaches), Maida Hill	1926	17.1.34	10.34

STAR (4)

	Reg	Model	Builder	Body	Operator	Year	In	Out
	JB292	Flyer VB4	Not known	B20F	A.F. & A.J. Moore (Imperial Bus Service), Windsor	1932	21.12.33	25.9.34
	MT1973	Flyer	Duple	C20D	A.T. Locke (Blue Saloon Coaches) via Aldershot & District	1929	† 12.1.38	29.3.38
	RO8852	Flyer VB4	United	B20F	A.R. Blowers (Express Motor Service), St Albans	1928	'2.1.34	10.34
	RO9027	Flyer VB4	Not known	B20F	A.R. Blowers (Express Motor Service), St Albans	1928	2.1.34	10.34

† Taken into stock unlicensed and never operated.

THORNYCROFT (25)

	Reg	Model	Builder	Body	Operator	Year	In	Out
n	JH49	A12	Thurgood	B20F	Peoples Motor Services Ltd, Ware	1931	1.12.33	7.5.36
n	JH1586	A12	Thurgood	B20F	Peoples Motor Services Ltd, Ware	1932	1.12.33	4.5.38
n	JH2054	A12	Thurgood	B20F	Peoples Motor Services Ltd, Ware	1932	1.12.33	4.5.38
n	UR7141	A2L	Thurgood	B20F	Peoples Motor Services Ltd, Ware	1930	1.12.33	4.5.38
n	UR7142	A2L	Thurgood	B20F	Peoples Motor Services Ltd, Ware	1930	1.12.33	3.5.38
n	UR7353	A2L	Thurgood	B20F	Peoples Motor Services Ltd, Ware	1930	1.12.33	3.5.38

n	UR7736	A2L	Thurgood	B20F	Peoples Motor Services Ltd, Ware	1930	1.12.33	7.4.36
n	UR7968	A2L	Thurgood	B20F	Peoples Motor Services Ltd, Ware	1930	1.12.33	18.4.36
n	UR9176	A2L	Thurgood	B20F	Peoples Motor Services Ltd, Ware	1931	1.12.33	3.5.38
n1	UV4086	BC	Vickers	C22R	London General Country Services (formerly Great Western Railway)	1929	1.7.33	10.34
n1	UV4087	BC	Vickers	C22R	London General Country Services (formerly Great Western Railway)	1929	1.7.33	10.34
n1	UV4088	BC	Vickers	C22R	London General Country Services (formerly Great Western Railway)	1929	1.7.33	10.34
	JH1587	Cygnet	Thurgood	B32F	Peoples Motor Services Ltd, Ware	1932	1.12.33	8.4.36
	JH3338	Cygnet	Thurgood	B26F	Peoples Motor Services Ltd, Ware	1932	1.7.33	15.5.36
	JH3432	Cygnet	Thurgood	B32F	Peoples Motor Services Ltd, Ware	1932	1.12.33	7.4.36
	KO9092	A2L	Not known	B20F	West Kent Motor Services Ltd	1928	† 4.10.39	2.1.40
	OT7822	LB	Not known	B29F	London General Country Services Ltd (formerly Woking & District)	1928	1.7.33	7.1.36
	PG1099	A2L	Challands Ross	B20F	London General Country Services Ltd (formerly Woking & District)	1929	1.7.33	23.4.36
	PG1757	BC	Challands Ross	B32R	London General Country Services Ltd (formerly Woking & District)	1929	1.7.33	23.4.36
	PG1758	BC	Challands Ross	B32R	London General Country Services Ltd (formerly Woking & District)	1929	1.7.33	10.4.36
	PG2018	A2L	Challands Ross	B20F	London General Country Services Ltd (formerly Woking & District)	1929	1.7.33	23.4.36
	PG3236	A2L	Challands Ross	B20F	London General Country Services Ltd (formerly Woking & District)	1929	1.7.33	23.4.36
	PG4226	A2L	Challands Ross	B20F	London General Country Services Ltd (formerly Woking & District)	1929	1.7.33	17.4.36
	VB4550	A2L	Wilton	B20F	London General Country Services Ltd (formerly Woking & District)	1929	1.7.33	6.1.36
	EKP140	Dainty	Thurgood	B20F	West Kent Motor Services Ltd	1938	† 4.10.39	2.1.40

n   Numbered NY 1–9 n1   Numbered TH 1–3
†   Taken into stock unlicensed and never operated

TILLING STEVENS (vehicles not included in LGOC O class) (11)

KM3864	B9A	Short Bros	B31R	Maidstone & District Motor Services Ltd	1926	1.7.33	5.35
KM3866	B9A	Short Bros	B31R	Maidstone & District Motor Services Ltd	1926	1.7.33	10.4.36
KO127	B9A	Short Bros	Ch31	Maidstone & District Motor Services Ltd	1927	1.7.33	10.34
KO131	B9A	Short Bros	Ch31	Maidstone & District Motor Services Ltd	1927	1.7.33	10.34
KP2558	B9B	Short Bros	B20F	West Kent Motor Services Ltd	1928	† 4.10.39	19.1.40
KP3003	B10A	Short Bros	C31R	Maidstone & District Motor Services Ltd	1929	1.7.33	10.34
KP3034	B10A	Harrington	C29R	Maidstone & District Motor Services Ltd	1929	1.7.33	10.34
PG9381	B10A2	Petty	B32D	London General Country Services Ltd (formerly Woking & District)	1930	1.7.33	10.4.36
RO9922	B10A2	Strachan	C32?	A. Barnes (Reliance Coaches), St Albans	1928	6.2.34	10.4.36
UL7939	B9A	Duple	C28?	C.E. Holmes (West London Coaches), Maida Hill	1929	17.1.34	9.4.36
UL7940	B9A	Duple	C28?	C.E. Holmes (West London Coaches), Maida Hill	1929	17.1.34	10.4.36

†   Taken into stock unlicensed and never operated

W & G (3)

GD2091	L	Not known	B26?	London General Country Services Ltd (formerly Watford O. Co.)	1926	1.7.33	3.34
GM983	L	Not known	B26?	Charles Russett & Son (St Albans & District)	1926	10.11.33	10.34
VA5567	L	Not known	B26F	Charles Russett & Son (St Albans & District)	1926	10.11.33	4.34